Ivy Global

SSAT

MATH

EDITION 2.0

IVY GLOBAL, NEW YORK

*SSAT is a registered trademark of the Secondary School Admission Test Board which is not affiliated with and does not endorse this product.

SSAT Math, Edition 2.0

This publication was written and edited by the team at Ivy Global.

Editor-in-Chief: Laurel Perkins
Layout Editor: Sacha Azor
Producers: Lloyd Min and Junho Suh

Contributors: Alexandra Candib, Isabel Carlin, Corwin Henville, Lei Huang, Nathan Létourneau, Mark Mendola, Sarah Pike, Yolanda Song, and Isabel Villeneuve

About Ivy Global

Ivy Global is a pioneering education company that provides a wide range of educational services.

E-mail: info@ivyglobal.com
Website: http://www.ivyglobal.com

Contents

Introduction

How to Use this Book 3

About the SSAT 5

Test-Taking Strategies

Approaching the SSAT 13

Math Strategies

Introduction 29

Basic Strategies 33

If You Get Stuck 39

Math Review

Introduction 49

Arithmetic 51

    Numbers and Operations 53

    Factors and Multiples 71

    Fractions 77

    Ratios 85

    Decimals 91

    Percents 97

    Word Problems 105

    Negative Numbers 113

    Exponents and Roots 119

    Order of Operations 125

    Arithmetic Review 129

Algebra 141

    Basic Algebra 143

    Expressions 149

    Equations 157

    Inequalities 163

    Strange Symbols 169

    Word Problems and Algebra 173

    Algebra Review 179

Geometry 191

    Lines and Angles 193

    Polygons 205

    Circles 219

    Solid Geometry 225

    Coordinate Geometry 239

    Geometry Review 255

Data Interpretation 271

    Charts and Graphs 273

    Range, Mean, Median, and Mode 285

    Probability 293

    Data Interpretation Review 303

Answers

    Arithmetic 323

    Algebra 335

    Geometry 339

    Data Interpretation 343

Introduction

Chapter 1

Section 1
How to Use this Book

Welcome, students and parents! This book is intended for students preparing for the Math section of the Middle or Upper Level Secondary School Admission Test (SSAT). For students applying to many top private and independent schools in North America, the SSAT is a crucial and sometimes daunting step in the admissions process. By leading you step-by-step through the fundamental content and most effective strategies for the SSAT, Ivy Global will help you build your confidence and maximize your score on this important exam.

This book is right for you if:

- you are applying to a private or independent school that requires the SSAT for admission
- you will be in Grades 5-7 (Middle Level) or 8-11 (Upper Level) when you take the SSAT
- you would like to learn and practice the best strategies for the Math section of the SSAT
- you are a parent, family member, or tutor looking for new ways to help your Middle or Upper-Level SSAT student

We know that no two students are exactly alike—each student brings a unique combination of personal strengths and weaknesses to his or her test preparation. For this reason, we've tailored our preparation materials to help students with a specific subject area or goal. Ivy Global's *SSAT Math* walks students through the best strategies for the SSAT Math sections, and provides thorough review and practice for all of the math concepts tested at each level. This book includes:

- an up-to-date introduction to the SSAT's administration, format, and scoring practices
- targeted strategies for students new to standardized tests, including study schedules, pacing, and stress management
- a complete introduction to the SSAT Math section, explaining in detail what concepts are tested and what types of questions are asked
- the most effective strategies for the SSAT Math section, including advanced strategies for Upper Level students
- a thorough review of all of the fundamental math concepts you will need to know for the SSAT, including arithmetic, algebra, geometry, and data interpretation

- online video tutorials for engaging additional explanations of each topic
- over 1,000 practice questions and drills, grouped into targeted practice sets for each concept and difficulty level

Work through the material that is appropriate to your level. If you are a Middle Level student, work through all of the material except any content marked "Upper Level." If you are an Upper Level student, review all of the basic material before you look at the "Upper Level" content. The two exams have the same basic format, so both younger and older students will benefit from learning the same basic strategies.

Finally, keep in mind that every student has a different learning style. If you come across a strategy or a concept that you find challenging, circle it and move on. You might find that some of the other strategies work better for you, and that is okay! Pick the strategies that are the best fit for your learning style and add them to your toolkit for taking the SSAT. You can always come back to more difficult material with the help of a trusted adult or tutor.

To get started, continue reading for an overview of the SSAT and some general test-taking advice. Good luck in this exciting new step for your education!

Section 2
About the SSAT

The **SSAT (Secondary School Admission Test)** is a standardized test administered to students in grades 3-11 to help determine placement into certain private and independent schools. Many secondary schools worldwide use the SSAT as an integral part of their admissions process. The SSAT is owned, published, and developed by the Secondary School Admission Test Board. All tests are printed in English.

You will register for one of three SSAT tests, depending on your grade level:
- The **Elementary Level** exam is for students currently in grades 3-4.
- The **Middle Level** exam (formerly Lower Level) is for students currently in grades 5-7.
- The **Upper Level** exam is for students currently in grades 8-11.

All levels have the same basic format but vary in difficulty and length. The Elementary Level is shorter than the Middle and Upper Levels.

When is the Test Administered?

The SSAT is administered at national test centers on "**Standard**" dates eight times during the academic year. In some locations, regional private schools and organizations also have the option of administering the test independently on non-standard dates. These independent dates are called "**Flex**" test dates, and they are listed by region on the SSAT website at www.ssat.org. It does not matter whether you take the exam on a Standard or Flex test date if both are offered in your location.

How Many Times Can I Take the Test?

In most locations, a student can register for a Standard test as often as desired, up to eight times per academic year. However, a student can only register for a Flex test once per academic year. For students applying to schools in Ontario, the Ontario Testing Consortium allows students to register for only one SSAT test per academic year. Any subsequent attempts to take the exam will be considered invalid and will not be reported to schools.

How Do I Register?

The easiest and fastest way to register is to complete the **online application**. Visit www.ssat.org to register for an exam in your location. The other alternative is to mail or fax a completed form to SSAT by the regular registration deadline.

Make sure to print off and keep the **Admission Ticket** that is obtainable only after the Secondary School Admission Test Board has received and processed your registration and payment. This ticket both serves as a confirmation for your test registration, and includes important details of your pending test: date, location of scheduled test, specific instructions regarding taking the SSAT, and your list of schools and consultants chosen to receive your SSAT scores.

What is the Format of the SSAT?

The SSAT consists of three main sections (**Verbal**, **Math**, and **Reading**), plus a **Writing Sample** that either takes the form of a creative writing assignment or an essay. The format of the test differs based on the level of the exam:

Elementary Level			
Section	Questions	Length	Topics Covered
Math	30 questions	30 min	Arithmetic, geometry, word problems
Verbal	30 questions	20 min	Vocabulary: synonyms and analogies
15-minute break			
Reading	28 questions	30 min	Short passages: fiction, non-fiction, poetry
Writing	1 prompt	15 min	Creative writing assignment (not scored)
Total testing time: 1 hour, 50 minutes			

Middle and Upper Levels			
Section	Questions	Length	Topics Covered
Writing	One prompt	25 min	Creative writing assignment or essay (not scored)
5-minute break			
Math I	25 questions	30 min	Arithmetic, algebra, geometry, word problems
Reading	40 questions	40 min	Short passages: fiction, non-fiction, poetry
10-minute break			
Verbal	60 questions	30 min	Vocabulary: synonyms and analogies
Math II	25 questions	30 min	Arithmetic, algebra, geometry, word problems
Experimental Section	16 questions	15 min	Varies: this section is testing out questions for upcoming years and is not scored
Total testing time: 3 hours, 5 minutes			

Except for the Writing Sample, all questions are **multiple choice** (A) to (E). You are not allowed to use calculators, rulers, dictionaries, or other aids during the exam.

How is the SSAT Scored?

All of the multiple-choice questions on the SSAT are equal in value, and your **raw score** for these sections is calculated as follows:

- One mark is given for every question answered correctly.
- $\frac{1}{4}$ mark is deducted for every question answered incorrectly.
- No marks are awarded or deducted for questions left blank.

Therefore, your raw score is the number of questions you answer correctly subtracted by one quarter point for each question you answer incorrectly.

Your raw score is then converted into a **scaled score** for each section (Verbal, Math, and Reading) that represents how well you did in comparison to the other students taking the same exam:

- Elementary Level scaled score: 300-600 for each section, 900-1800 total
- Middle Level scaled score: 440-710 for each section, 1320-2130 total
- Upper Level scaled score: 500-800 for each section, 1500-2400 total

The **Writing Sample** is not scored, but is sent to the schools you are applying to as a sample of your writing skills. Admissions officers may use your essay or story to evaluate your writing ability when they are making admissions decisions.

The **Experimental Section** on the Middle and Upper Levels is the SSAT's method of testing out new questions for upcoming years. The section is not scored, but students should try to complete it to the best of their ability. The section may include any mixture of Verbal, Reading, or Math questions.

Scores are released to families and to the schools that families have designated as recipients within two weeks after the test date. Schools receive a printed report by mail and an electronic copy online. Families receive an electronic copy and can request a printed report for an extra fee. You may designate certain schools as recipients during registration, or at any time before or after testing through your online account at www.ssat.org.

What are the SSAT Percentiles?

The SSAT score report also provides **SSAT percentile** rankings for each category, comparing your performance to that of other students in the same grade who have taken the test in the past three years. If you score in the 60th percentile, this means you scored higher than 60% of other students in your grade taking the exam.

These percentile rankings provide a more accurate way of evaluating student performance at each grade level. However, the SSAT percentiles only compare your score to those of other students who have taken the SSAT, and these tend to be very high-achieving students. Students should not be discouraged if their percentile rankings appear low.

Because the Elementary Level exam was first administered in 2012, percentile data for this test has not yet been released.

Median Scores (SSAT 50th Percentile)				
	Grade	Reading	Verbal	Quantitative
Middle Level	5	585	590	587
	6	603	610	611
	7	628	635	635
Upper Level	8	647	660	676
	9	653	667	699
	10	659	670	705
	11	647	656	704

The SSAT also publishes an Estimated National Percentile Ranking for test takers in grades 5-9, which provides an estimated comparison of student performance against the entire national student population, not just the set of students taking the SSAT. The test also provides a projected SAT score for test-takers in grades 7-10.

How Do Schools Use the SSAT?

Schools use the SSAT as one way to assess potential applicants, but it is by no means the only tool that they are using. Schools also pay very close attention to the rest of the student's application—academic record, teacher recommendations, extracurricular activities, writing samples, and interviews—in order to determine which students might be the best fit for their program. The personal components of a student's application give schools a lot more information about the student's personality and potential contributions to the school's overall community. Different schools place a different amount of importance on SSAT and other test scores within this process; admissions offices are good places to find how much your schools of interest will weigh the SSAT.

Test-Taking Strategies
Chapter 2

Section 1
Approaching the SSAT

Before you review the content covered on the SSAT, you need to focus on *how* you take the SSAT. If you approach the SSAT *thoughtfully* and *strategically*, you will avoid common traps and tricks planted in the SSAT by the test makers. Think of the SSAT as a timed maze—you need to make every turn cleverly and quickly so that you avoid getting stuck at a dead end with no time to spare.

In this section, you will learn about the SSAT's format and structure; this awareness will help you avoid any surprises or shocks on test day. The SSAT is a very predictable exam and will seem less challenging once you understand what it looks like and how it works. By learning strategies and techniques for best test-taking practice, you will discover how to work as quickly and intelligently as possible. Once you know what to expect, you can refine your knowledge of the content tested on the SSAT, such as the verbal and math skills that are based on your grade level in school.

This section on SSAT strategies will answer your major questions:

- How does the SSAT differ from a test you take in school?
- What preparation strategies can you learn before you take the SSAT?
- What strategies can you learn to use during the SSAT?
- How can you manage stress before and during the SSAT?

In the process of answering your big questions, this section will also highlight key facts about smart test-taking:

- Your answer choice matters—your process does not. Grid your answer choices correctly and carefully to earn points. You have a set amount of time per section, so spend it wisely.
- The SSAT's format and directions do not change, so learn them now.
- All questions have the same value.
- Each level of the SSAT corresponds to a range of grades, and score expectations differ based on your grade level.
- Identify your areas of strength and weakness, and review any content that feels unfamiliar.

- Apply universal strategies—prediction-making, Process of Elimination, back-solving, and educated guessing—to the multiple-choice sections.
- Stay calm and be confident in your abilities as you prepare for and take the SSAT.

How Does the SSAT Differ from a Test You Take in School?

Part 1

The SSAT differs from assessments you take in school in four major ways:

1. It is not concerned with the process behind your answers. Your answer is either right or wrong; there is no partial credit.
2. You have a set amount of time per section (and for the exam as a whole).
3. It is divided into three levels that correspond to three grade ranges of students.
4. It is extremely predictable given that its format, structure, and directions never vary.

No Partial Credit

At this point in your school career, you have probably heard your teacher remark, "Be sure to show your work on the test!" You are most likely familiar with almost every teacher's policy of "No work, no credit." However, the SSAT completely ignores this guideline. The machine that grades your exam does not care that you penciled brilliant logic in the margins of the test booklet—the machine only looks at your gridded answer choice. Your answer choice is either right or wrong; **there is no partial credit**.

Set Amount of Time

You have a **set amount of time per section**, so spend it wisely. The SSAT test proctors will never award you extra time after a test section has ended because you spent half of one section struggling valiantly on a single problem. Instead, you must learn to work within each section's time constraints.

You also must view the questions as equal because **each question is worth one point**. Even though some questions are more challenging than others, they all carry the same weight. Rather than dwell on a problem, you should skip it, work through the rest of the section, and come back to it if you have time.

Three Levels

There are three levels of the SSAT—Elementary, Middle, and Upper—each of which is administered to a specific range of students. The Elementary Level is given to students in grades 3 and 4; the Middle Level is given to students in grades 5, 6, and 7; and the Upper Level is given to students in grades 8, 9, 10, and 11. While you might be used to taking tests in school that are completely tailored to your grade, the SSAT is different: each test level covers content from a specific range of grade levels.

Score expectations differ based on your grade level. You are not expected to answer as many questions correctly on a Middle Level exam if you are only in fifth grade. Conversely, if you are in seventh grade, you are expected to answer the most questions correctly on the Middle Level exam because you are one of the oldest students taking that exam.

Standard Format

The SSAT is, by definition, a **standardized test**, which means that its format and directions are standard and predictable. While your teachers might change formats and directions for every assessment they administer, you can expect to see the same format and directions on every SSAT.

What Preparation Strategies Can You Learn Before You Take the SSAT?

Part 2

Now that you are familiar with how the SSAT differs from the tests you take in school, you are ready to learn some test tips. You can prepare for the SSAT by following these three steps:

- Learn the format and directions of the test.
- Identify your areas of strength and weakness.
- Create a study schedule to review and practice test content.

Learn the Format and Directions

The structure of the SSAT is entirely predictable, so learn this now. Rather than wasting precious time reading the directions and understanding the format on test day, take the time now to familiarize yourself with the test's format and directions.

Refer to the tables on page 6 and 7 for an overview of the SSAT's format. Specific directions for the Verbal, Reading, and Writing sections can be found in Ivy Global's *SSAT English*. Specific directions for the math section can be found in Ivy Global's *SSAT Math*.

Identify Your Strengths and Weaknesses

To determine your areas of strength and weakness and identify which concepts you need to review, take a full-length, accurate practice exam to serve as a diagnostic test. Four full-length practice exams can be found in this book: two for the Middle Level and two for the Upper Level.

Make sure you simulate test day conditions by timing yourself. Then, check your answers against the correct answers. Write down how many questions you missed in each section, and note the topics or types of questions you found most challenging (e.g. analogies, fiction passages, geometry, or data analysis). What was hard about the test? What did you feel good about? Did you leave a lot of questions blank because of timing issues, or did you leave questions blank because you did not know how to solve them? Reflecting on these questions, in addition to looking at your score breakdown, will help you determine your strengths, weaknesses, and areas for improvement.

Create a Study Schedule

After determining your areas of strength and weakness, create a study plan and schedule for your SSAT preparation to review content. Work backward from your test date until you arrive at your starting point for studying. The number of weeks you have until your exam will determine how much time you can (and should) devote to your preparation. Remember, practice is the most important thing!

To begin, try using this sample study plan as a model for your own personalized study schedule.

Sample Study Plan

My test date is: _____.

I have _____ weeks to study. I will make an effort to study _____ minutes/hours every day/week, and I will set aside extra time on _____ to take timed sections.

I plan to take _____ full-length tests between now and my test date. I will study for _____ weeks and then take a practice test. My goal for this test is to improve my score in the following specific areas:

_____

_____

_____

_____

_____

_____

_____

_____

_____

_____

If I do not make this goal, then I will spend more time studying.

Study Schedule				
Date	Plan of Study	Time Allotted	Time Spent	Goal Reached?
1/1	Learn 5 words and review perimeter of polygons	1 hour	44 minutes	Yes, I know 5 new words and can calculate perimeter!
1/3	Learn 5 words and review area of triangles	1 hour	1 hour	I know 5 new words, but I'm still confused about the area of triangles. I'll review this again next time and ask a teacher, tutor, or parent for help.

What Strategies Can You Learn to Use During the Test?

Part 3

Once you have grown accustomed to the SSAT through practice, you are ready to learn strategies to use during the SSAT. The following points will prepare you to take the test as cleverly and efficiently as possible:

- Grid your answer choices correctly and carefully.
- Pace yourself to manage your time effectively.
- Learn a strategic approach for multiple-choice questions.

Gridding Answer Choices

For the Middle and Upper Level exams, you must enter your answers on a separate answer sheet. In school you probably take tests that, for the most part, do not ask you to transfer your answers to a separate sheet. However, the SSAT streamlines the grading process by only reviewing your answer sheet. You must grid in your multiple-choice answers onto this sheet using an HB pencil to fill in the circle that corresponds to your answer. This sheet is scanned and scored by a highly sensitive computer. You will also write your Writing Sample on separate lined pages of this answer sheet.

Since you have to take an additional step to record your answers, it is important that you avoid making gridding mistakes. Sadly, many students get confused and mismark their answer sheets. Remember, even if you arrive at the right answer, it is only correct and counted in your favor if you grid correctly on your answer sheet.

To grid correctly and carefully to maximize your points, consider the following tips:

Keep your answer sheet neat. Since your answer sheet is graded by a machine, your score is calculated based on what your marks look like. The machine cannot know what you really meant if you picked the wrong bubble. Stray marks can harm your score, especially if you darken the correct answer but accidentally make a mark that confuses the machine! Avoid this and other errors by consulting the following image, which shows the difference between answers that are properly shaded and those that are not.

1. Ⓐ Ⓑ Ⓒ Ⓓ Ⓔ ✗   Answer 1 is wrong because no answer is selected and there are stray marks.

2. Ⓐ Ⓑ Ⓒ Ⓓ Ⓔ ✗   Answer 2 is neither right nor wrong because it was left blank.

3. Ⓐ Ⓑ Ⓒ Ⓓ Ⓔ ✗   Answer 3 is wrong because two answers have been selected.

4. Ⓐ Ⓑ Ⓒ Ⓓ Ⓔ ✗   Answer 4 is wrong because two answers have been selected.

5. Ⓐ Ⓑ Ⓒ Ⓓ Ⓔ ✗   Answer 5 is wrong because choice (E) has not been darkened properly and there are stray marks.

6. Ⓐ Ⓑ Ⓒ Ⓓ Ⓔ ✓   Answer 6 is right because choice (A) has been darkened properly.

Train yourself to **circle your answer choice in your test booklet**. If you have time to go back and check your answers, you can easily check your circled answers against your gridded ones.

You should also **create a system for marking questions that you skipped** or that you found confusing (see the next section for more information about skipping around). Try circling those question numbers only in your test booklet so that you can find them if you want to solve them later or check your work. Be aware of these questions when gridding answers on your answer sheet.

Finally, **grid your answers in batches of four, five, or six answer choices.** That way, you do not have to go back and forth between your test booklet and your answer sheet every minute. If you choose to use this strategy, keep an eye on the clock—you do not want to get to the end of the section and find you have not gridded any answers. Depending on how much time you have left to check your work (if you happen to finish early), you can either review every problem or spot-check a series of questions on your answer sheet against your test booklet.

Time Management (Pacing)

Manage your time effectively to boost your score. Just as effective gridding contributes to time management, other strategies enable you to work efficiently and maximize the number of problems you answer. Specifically, skipping questions is particularly important because you need to learn to keep moving on the exam rather than wasting too much time on any single question.

You can skip questions within each section of the SSAT; the freedom to skip questions is helpful since each question is worth only one point. If you are stuck on a problem, you should move on after a minute or two and try to answer another problem. It makes more sense to answer as many questions as possible (and get as many points as possible) rather than spending all your time on one question. If you come across a question you want to skip, mark it in your question booklet (by circling it, underlining it, etc.) and move to the next question; just be sure to skip the corresponding number on your answer sheet if you choose to skip a question. Remember not to make any stray marks on your answer sheet.

There is a benefit to skipping questions. By moving quickly through each question of the section, you will ensure that: 1) you see every question in the section; 2) you gain points on questions that are easy for you; 3) you return to more challenging problems and hopefully answer as many as you can with your remaining time. It is also important to note that you might not be able to answer several questions in each section if you are on the younger end of the testing group for your particular test level. In that case, you should skip those questions unless you can eliminate one or more answer choices. Also, think about the value of skipping in terms of the guessing penalty. If you cannot make a clever guess on a hard problem, then you should skip it and move on because choosing a random answer will most likely cause you to lose one quarter of a point.

Follow this step-by-step process to decide when to skip questions:

1. Look through the section and answer the questions that are easy for you first. Circle any questions that you are not sure about or seem harder.
2. After answering all the easier questions, go back to the questions you have circled and spend some time working on ones that you think you might be able to solve.
3. Skip any questions that you have no idea how to solve.

Continue reading for more detailed information about the guessing penalty and guessing strategies.

Strategies for Multiple-Choice Questions

Apply universal strategies—prediction-making, Process of Elimination, back-solving, and educated guessing—to the multiple-choice sections. To illustrate the value of these strategies, read through the following example of a synonym question from the Verbal Section:

Example

HAPPY:

(A) delighted
(B) unhappy
(C) crazy
(D) nice
(E) depressed

Answer: (A). "Delighted" is the correct answer because it is the word that most nearly means "happy."

Regardless of whether the answer choices are easy, difficult, or somewhere in between, you can use certain tricks and tips to your advantage. To approach SSAT questions effectively, you need to step into the test makers' minds and learn to use their traps against them.

Make predictions. When you see a question, try to come up with an answer on your own before looking at the answer choices. You can literally cover the answer choices with your hand so that you must rely on your own intelligence to predict an answer instead of being swayed by answer choices that you see. If you look at the answer choices first, you might be tempted to circle a choice without thinking about the other options and what the question is asking you. Instead, make a prediction so that you understand the question fully and get a clear sense of what to look for in the answers. In the synonym example above, you could predict that a possible synonym for "happy" would be something like "glad."

Use the **Process of Elimination**. For each multiple-choice question, the answer is always right in front of you. To narrow down your answer choices, actively identify obviously incorrect answers and eliminate them. Even if you can eliminate just one answer, you will set yourself up for better odds if you decide to guess. For the synonym example above, test your prediction of "glad" against the answer choices and immediately eliminate "unhappy" and "depressed" since they are nearly opposite in meaning. You can also probably eliminate "crazy" and "nice" since those words do not match your prediction as well as "delighted," which is the correct answer.

Try back-solving. This strategy is most useful on the math sections, especially when you are given a complicated, multi-step word problem. Instead of writing an equation, try plugging in the answer choices to the word problem. Take a look at the following question:

Example

Catherine has a basket of candy. On Monday, she eats ½ of all the candy. On Tuesday, she eats 2 pieces. On Wednesday, she eats twice the amount of candy that she consumed on Tuesday. If she only has 4 pieces left on Thursday, how many pieces did she initially have?

(A) 12
(B) 14
(C) 16
(D) 20
(E) 22

To use back-solving, start with answer choice (C) and plug it into the word problem. If (C) is the correct answer, you are done. If not, you will then know whether you should test (B) or (D). On the SSAT, numerical answer options are always listed in either ascending or descending order, from least to greatest or from greatest to least, meaning that even if (C) is incorrect, you will then be able to identify whether your answer should be larger or smaller than (C); you can then test (B) or (D) accordingly.

When we start with 16 pieces of candy, we subtract 8 on Monday, then 4 more for Tuesday, and then 2 more for Wednesday. By Thursday, Catherine only has two pieces of candy left, which is less than the amount we wanted. Therefore, we know our answer has to be bigger, so we eliminate choices (A), (B), and (C) and try (D), which works.

(*Fun Fact:* If you think about it, you will only ever have to plug in three answer choices at most to determine the right answer.)

Use educated guessing. Before taking any test, it is important to understand the test's grading rules for correct answers, incorrect answers, and blank answers. The SSAT has a **wrong-answer penalty** for all three levels of the test, which means:

- You lose one quarter of a point from your total score for each question you answer incorrectly.
- You receive one point for every question you answer correctly.
- If you leave a question blank, you do not lose points—but you do not gain points either (so your score will not reach the highest possible range).

The SSAT's penalty is often referred to as a guessing penalty since its purpose is to discourage random guessing. If you did not lose points for guessing, then you could possibly pick the same answer choice for an entire section and get twenty percent of the questions—or more—correct. Thus, the guessing penalty is important because it makes sure your score reflects your abilities rather than your luck when guessing.

Guessing cleverly can certainly improve your score. If you can rule out one or two choices for a tricky question, then you should guess because your chances for guessing correctly are above average. However, if you cannot eliminate any of the answer choices, then guessing is not worth the risk of a quarter-point penalty. In that case, leave the answer blank and move on quickly to gain points on other questions.

Armed with these strategies, you might feel that SSAT is starting to look more manageable because you now have shortcuts that will help you navigate the maze of questions quickly and cleverly.

Take a look at this example to practice using the strategies you just read about.

Example

Doll is to toy as pasta is to

(A) mall
(B) Italy
(C) America
(D) dessert
(E) food

1. Assess the question and recognize what it is testing. In this case, the question tests whether you can complete the analogy.
2. Make a prediction. A doll is a type of toy, so pasta must be a type of something. How about "dinner"?

3. Look for inaccurate answer choices and eliminate them. "Mall" does not make sense. "Italy" and "America" both make pasta, but they are not examples of food or dinner. Dessert is a type of food, but pasta is not a dessert. "Food" is the only possible answer in this case.

4. Make an educated guess, or choose the best answer if you feel confident about it. Since you made a fantastic prediction and used Process of Elimination, you only have one choice left: (E). "Food" is the correct answer—you just earned yourself a point!

How Can You Manage Your Stress?
Part 4

It is natural to be nervous leading up to your exam. However, if that feeling starts to become overwhelming, here are some strategies that you can use. Many of these suggestions are good ideas to use in everyday life, but they become especially important in the final week before your test and on test day itself.

- **Relax and slow down.** To center yourself and ease your nerves, take a big, deep breath. Slowly inhale for a few seconds and then slowly exhale for a few seconds. Shut your eyes and relax. Stretch your arms, roll your neck gently, crack your knuckles—get in the zone of Zen! Continue to breathe deeply and slowly until you can literally feel your body calm down.
- **Picture your goals.** Close your eyes or just pause to reflect on what you want to achieve on test day. Visualize your success; acknowledge your former successes and abilities, and believe in yourself.
- **Break it down.** Instead of trying to study a whole section at once, break up your studying into small and manageable chunks. Outline your study goals before you start. For example, instead of trying to master the entire Reading Section at once, you might want to work on one type of passage at a time.
- **Sleep.** Make sure you get plenty of rest and sleep, especially the two nights leading up to your exam.
- **Fuel up.** Eat healthy, filling meals that fuel your brain. Also, drink lots of water to stay hydrated.
- **Take a break.** Put down the books and go play outside, read, listen to music, exercise, or talk to a trusted friend or family member. A good break can be just as restful as a nap. However, watching television will provide minimal relaxation.

On the night before the exam, study only lightly. Make a list of your three biggest fears and work on them, but don't try to learn anything new. Pick out what you are going to wear to the exam—try wearing layers in case the exam room is hotter or colder than you expect. Organize everything you need to bring, including your Admissions Ticket. Know where the test center is located and how long it will take to get there. Have a nutritious meal and get plenty of sleep!

On the morning of the exam, let your adrenaline kick in naturally. Eat a good breakfast and stay hydrated; your body needs fuel to endure the test. Bring along several pencils and a good eraser. Listen carefully to the test proctor's instructions and let the proctor know if you are left-handed so you can sit in an appropriate desk. Take a deep breath and remember: you are smart and accomplished! Believe in yourself and you will do just fine.

Math Strategies
Chapter 3

Section 1
Introduction

On the Middle and Upper Levels, the SSAT has two 30-minute Math sections with 25 multiple-choice questions each. Each multiple-choice question will have five answer options, (A) through (E), and you will need to pick the one that best answers the question. The questions will test your knowledge of arithmetic, algebra, geometry, and data interpretation. There will be a mixture of all four of these topics on each math section and you will need to apply your knowledge of these topics efficiently to solve problems with a strict time limit. Some of these problems will have multiple steps and will require you to apply many different skills. Calculators, rulers, compasses, protractors, and other aids are not permitted on the SSAT.

How to Approach the Math Section
Part 1

Pace Yourself

Start out with questions you can answer quickly, and circle questions that will take longer so you can come back to them later. Don't spend too long on one question, but don't rush yourself. If you find that you are spending too long on a particular question, circle it and come back to it at the end if you have more time. Remember that each question is worth only one point, so don't waste time struggling with a difficult question when you can answer three easier questions in the same amount of time.

Make Educated Guesses

You don't need to answer every question to get a good score. Remember that you are deducted one quarter-point for each incorrect answer. If you encounter a question that immediately seems too hard, circle it and come back later if you have more time. If you can definitely eliminate at least one of the five answer choices, it is better to guess than to leave the question blank. Your odds of guessing the correct answer increase with the more answers you can eliminate. Skip questions you have absolutely no idea how to answer.

Write Down Your Process

Write down your work on the scratch paper provided. Don't rely on mental math alone. It is easy to make a careless mistake when you are trying to remember numbers in your head.

Break complicated problems into steps and tackle one step at a time. Do you need to first find the area of a triangle, then the area of a square, and then compare the two using fractions? Write down these steps for yourself so you remember what to do next.

Use Figures and Diagrams

Figures provided by the SSAT are not necessarily drawn to scale. Trust and use the measurements that have been provided for these figures. Write in any other measurements that are given in the problem or that can be deduced from the information given.

Are you working on a geometry problem with no figure provided? Draw your own! Are you working with negative numbers? Draw a number line! Drawings can be very helpful for organizing your thoughts and information.

Check Your Work

If you have extra time, go back and check all of your work to make sure that you have not made any careless errors. Remember that there is no partial credit on this test—if you make an arithmetic mistake that causes you to get the wrong answer, you will not receive any points for that question.

Stay Calm

Understand that the same test is taken by students across a range of grade levels. This means that you might see material that you haven't learned yet in school. If you see a question that seems too hard for you, don't fret. Keep in mind that your scores will be compared with the scores of students at your same grade level. Chances are, if you find a question too difficult, most other test-takers your age will, too.

Review and Practice Math Concepts

Make sure you are comfortable with all of the exam concepts appropriate to your grade level, and spend some time reviewing the concepts you find challenging. In the Math Review later in this book, you will find explanations and practice questions for all of the concepts commonly tested on the SSAT. As you look at the Math Review, focus on reviewing concepts that are familiar to you before moving on to unfamiliar topics.

Section 2
Basic Strategies

Use this section to review some of the best test-taking strategies for the SSAT Math section. As you practice, keep in mind that not all problems are solved in the same manner. As a student with your own unique learning style, you may also find that some strategies work better for you than others. Try out all of the methods below, and identify the strategies that work best for you.

Most of the math questions on the SSAT are word problems, so your job is to find a way to convert the wording of these questions into math concepts that you can recognize. When you first encounter a problem, use the following steps to get started.

Read the Question Carefully

Read through the whole question. Don't assume you understand the question just by reading the first few words! Reading the whole question will help you avoid making assumptions that can lead to careless errors.

If you see unfamiliar or difficult-looking material, stay calm and keep reading until the end of the question. There might be more information in the question that will help you figure out the solution. If you still think a question is too difficult after you have finished reading the whole thing, then you should circle it in your question booklet, skip it, and come back to it if you have time. Don't be worried if you can't solve a question; not every student is expected to answer every question, and some questions might be beyond your grade level.

Here is a simple example that we will work through to demonstrate these basic test-taking strategies. Read the whole question carefully:

Example
A triangle has three sides with lengths 3, 4, and 5. What is the perimeter of the triangle?

(A) 3

(B) 7

(C) 9

(D) 12

(E) 15

Underline Key Words

Underline or circle any information given in the question that will help you solve it. Our example question should now look something like this:

A <u>triangle</u> has three sides with lengths <u>3, 4, and 5</u>. What is the <u>perimeter</u> of the triangle?

Identify What the Question is Asking

Ask yourself, "What is the question asking me to solve?" This is especially important for word problems. Sometimes the wording of a question can be confusing, so make it simpler for yourself and summarize in your own words what the question is asking for. Pay close attention to the key words you have underlined, and take a moment to remember their meanings as you summarize the question.

In our example question, you are being asked to find the perimeter of the triangle. This was one of the words we underlined in the question. To remind yourself that this is what the question is asking, you might want to underline this word again:

A <u>triangle</u> has three sides with lengths <u>3, 4, and 5</u>. What is the <u>perimeter</u> of the triangle?

How would you explain the "perimeter," in your own words? You might remember that the perimeter is the length of the outline of the triangle.

Draw a Chart or Diagram

Charts and diagrams are great tools to help you visualize the problem and organize your information. In our example question, you might try drawing a quick sketch of a triangle. Then, fill in any information you are given in the question. You can write in the lengths of all three sides:

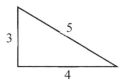

Come Up with a Strategy

Strategize the best way to solve the question. Sometimes finding the answer requires some thought if there are multiple steps involved. Think about all of the information provided in the question and how it is related. Think about where you have seen this type of question before, and what methods you have used to solve similar types of questions. If there is a formula that you know that could help, write it down. Here's a strategy we could use to solve our example question.

- *We know*: the lengths of the sides of the triangle are 3, 4, and 5.
- *We want*: the perimeter, which is the length of the outline of the triangle.
- *Our strategy*: add up the lengths of all three sides of the triangle.

$$perimeter = 3 + 4 + 5 = 12$$

Is our solution one of the answer choices? It is indeed! The answer is (D), 12.

Check Your Answer

Always check your work to make sure that you picked the best answer out of all of the options the SSAT gave you! Double-check all of your arithmetic to make sure that you didn't make any careless errors.

Make sure that you solved for what the question was asking. For example, if the question asked to solve for perimeter, make sure you didn't solve for area.

Try to determine whether or not your answer seems reasonable based on context. For example, if the length of one side of the triangle is 3, the perimeter cannot be 3, so answer (A) in our example is unreasonable.

Finally, check that you bubbled in the answer on your answer sheet correctly. It would be a shame to have solved the question correctly and not get credit!

Putting it All Together

Here is another example question that is a bit more complicated. Use the same question-solving steps to try it out.

1. **Read the question:**

   The width of a rectangular field is one-quarter its length. If the length is 16, what is the perimeter of the field?

   (A) 4
   (B) 24
   (C) 36
   (D) 40
   (E) 64

2. **Underline key words:**

   The <u>width</u> of a <u>rectangular</u> field is <u>one-quarter its length</u>. If the <u>length is 16</u>, what is the <u>perimeter</u> of the field?

3. **Ask yourself, "What is the question asking me to solve?"**

   Just like our first example, you are being asked to find the perimeter of the rectangle. Put this in your own words: the perimeter is the length of the outline of the rectangle.

4. **Draw a diagram:**

   Try drawing a quick sketch of a rectangle and fill in any information given in the question:

   $width = {}^1\!/_4\ length$

   $length = 16$

5. **Strategize a solution:**

   We know: *length* = 16

   $$width = \frac{1}{4} \text{ of } length = \frac{1}{4} \text{ of } 16 = \frac{1}{4} \times 16 = \frac{16}{4} = 4$$

We want: the perimeter of the whole rectangle

Our strategy: we can use a formula that relates a rectangle's perimeter to its length and width.

$$perimeter = (2 \times length) + (2 \times width)$$

We can now plug in the values and solve:

$$perimeter = (2 \times 16) + (2 \times 4) = 32 + 8 = 40$$

If you did not remember this formula, look at the diagram again. To find the perimeter, we need to add up the lengths of the four sides of the rectangle. Our sides include two lengths and two widths, so here's how we would add them up:

$$perimeter = 16 + 4 + 16 + 4 = 40$$

There are often many different ways to solve a problem, so think creatively to find a strategy that works for you!

Section 3
If You Get Stuck

If you are having trouble solving a problem mathematically, here are a few useful strategies. Try to use these strategies while doing practice exams so that you become familiar with them.

Process of Elimination
Part 1

It is worthwhile to guess on a question if you can eliminate any answer options that you know are wrong. So how do you eliminate wrong answers? Read the question and the answer choices, and determine whether any of them seem unreasonable. For example:

Example

Which of the following fractions is less than $1/3$?

(A) $4/18$

(B) $4/12$

(C) $3/3$

(D) $12/9$

(E) $12/4$

Even if you forget how to solve the question above, you can eliminate wrong answers. You know that $1/3$ is less than 1. Remember that an "improper fraction" has a numerator that is greater than its denominator, and any improper fraction is greater than 1. Because answers (D) and (E) are both improper fractions, they must be greater than 1, so they can't be less than $1/3$. You can eliminate both of those choices right away.

You might also remember that a fraction with the same numerator and denominator is always equal to 1. Answer (C) has the same numerator and denominator, so it must be equal to 1 and can't be less than $1/3$. You can also eliminate answer (C).

If you don't know how to proceed with the arithmetic, you can guess between (A) and (B) and you will have pretty good odds of getting the correct answer. Or, you can look at answer (B) and reduce $4/12$ to $1/3$. Because the question is asking for a fraction that is less than $1/3$, (B) can't be the correct answer. You are left with only one possible answer: (A).

Guess and Check
Part 2

Sometimes you can narrow your choices down to one based on what seems reasonable, and then check to see if this is actually the correct answer. This is often true with geometry questions or problems where a diagram is given. For example:

Example

Julia arrived at Jenny's house at 6:35 PM. Her mother picked her up at 8:04 PM. How long did Julia spend at Jenny's house?

(A) 29 minutes

(B) 1 hour, 9 minutes

(C) 1 hour, 29 minutes

(D) 2 hours, 9 minutes

(E) 2 hours, 29 minutes

We can guess an answer for this question by rounding the times. 6:35 PM is approximately 6:30 PM and 8:04 PM is approximately 8:00 PM. The time between 6:30 to 7:00 is half an hour, and the time from 7:00 to 8:00 is another hour. Therefore, the time between 6:30 to 8:00 is about an hour and a half.

Looking at the answer choices, this is very close to (C) 1 hour, 29 minutes, so you can guess that this is the right answer. If you're running out of time, you might want to circle (C) as your best guess and move on.

In order to check that (C) is actually the right answer, subtract 6:35 PM from 8:04 PM:

$$\begin{array}{r} 8{:}04 \\ -\ 6{:}35 \\ \hline \end{array}$$

8 hours and 4 minutes is the same as 7 hours and 64 minutes. Use borrowing and re-write 8:04 as 7:64 so you can subtract properly:

$$\begin{array}{r} 7{:}64 \\ -\ 6{:}35 \\ \hline 1{:}29 \end{array}$$

Using subtraction, we can see that the answer is 1:29, or (C). Our estimation by rounding was close to the actual answer, and our guess was correct.

Now, try the guess-and-check method for a more challenging question:

Figure *PQRS* (drawn to scale) is a square with side lengths of 12. What is the area of the shaded region?

(A) 50

(B) 72

(C) 100

(D) 120

(E) It cannot be determined from the information given.

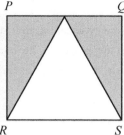

Because *PQRS* is a square, its area is $12 \times 12 = 144$. We're told that the diagram is drawn to scale, and it looks like that the shaded area is approximately half of the area of the square. Based on this estimate, let's see if we can eliminate any answers that seem unreasonable. Answer (D) is too large, and so is (C). (A) seems too small because 50 is about $\frac{1}{3}$ of 144. (B) seems about right, so we can circle (B) as our best guess.

Now we can check to see if (B) is actually correct. The area of the unshaded triangle is $\frac{1}{2} \times \text{base} \times \text{height} = \frac{1}{2} (12)(12) = \frac{1}{2} (144) = 72$. Subtract this from the area of the square to find the shaded area: $144 - 72 = 72$.

Our initial estimate was exactly right! If you were short on time and didn't have time to check all of the calculations for this problem, you would have been correct with this guess.

Picking Numbers

Sometimes an algebra question may seem difficult or abstract because it contains a lot of **variables**—letters or symbols that stand for numbers. The quickest way to solve these questions is to simplify the algebra. However, you can also make any question more concrete by picking an easy number to work with and plugging in this number instead of a variable.

The "picking numbers" method is typically used to solve questions whose answer choices are algebraic expressions. For example, you might be asked to state someone's age or height "in terms of" variables, remainders, percentages, or fractions of variables. You might also be asked to determine whether an expression or variable is even or odd. Both of these situations are excellent times to use the "picking numbers" method. For example:

Example

Michelle is 3 years older than Tommy. If Tommy is t years old, then how old is Michelle, in terms of t?

(A) $t + 3$

(B) $t - 3$

(C) $3t$

(D) $t \div 3$

(E) $3 - t$

This example has variables in the answer choices, so we can use the "picking numbers" method. Pick an age for Tommy to replace t. Let's pick 10. (You could have chosen any number, because algebraic expressions must be true no matter what number replaces the variable.) If Tommy is 10 years old, Michelle is 3 years older than Tommy, so Michelle is $10 + 3 = 13$ years old. The next step is to replace t with Tommy's age (10) in each of the answer choices:

(A) $10 + 3 = 13$

(B) $10 - 3 = 7$

(C) $3 \times 10 = 30$

(D) $10 \div 3 = 3\frac{1}{3}$

(E) $3 - 10 = -7$

If Tommy is 10 years old, we've already determined that Michelle must be 13 years old. Therefore, answer (A) is correct.

Let's try another slightly more challenging example:

Example

Nathan is three inches taller than Joseph, who is five inches shorter than Ethan. If e represents Ethan's height in inches, then how many inches tall is Nathan, in terms of e?

(A) $e + 6$

(B) $e + 4$

(C) $e + 2$

(D) e

(E) $e - 2$

This example has variables in the answer choices, so we can apply the "picking numbers" method. Let's say that Ethan is 50 inches tall, so $e = 50$. (Remember that you can choose any number and this method will still work.) If Ethan is 50 inches tall, we know that Joseph is five inches shorter, so Joseph is $50 - 5 = 45$ inches tall. Nathan is three inches taller than Joseph, so he is $45 + 3 = 48$ inches tall.

The question is asking for Nathan's height in terms of e. The next step is to replace e with Ethan's height (50) into each of the answer choices, and figure out which one matches Nathan's height (48):

(A) $50 + 6 = 56$

(B) $50 - 4 = 54$

(C) $50 + 2 = 52$

(D) 50

(E) $50 - 2 = 48$

We know that Nathan's height is 48 inches when Ethan's height is 50 inches, so answer (E) is correct.

Back-Solving

Part 4

Back-solving is a method that allows you to work backwards from the multiple-choice answers you are given. Unlike the "picking numbers" method, you can only use back-solving if your answer choices don't include variables. When your answer choices are numbers, you can expect them to be given in order from largest to smallest or smallest to largest. Take the middle answer (C) and plug it into your problem. If it works, it is right. If not, you can usually determine whether to try a larger or smaller answer. For example:

Example

Two consecutive numbers have a sum of 13. What is the smaller of the two numbers?

(A) 5
(B) 6
(C) 7
(D) 8
(E) 9

Start with answer choice (C). If 7 is the smaller number, then the two consecutive numbers are 7 and 8, which have a sum of 15. The correct numbers must add up to 13, so we're looking for a starting number that is smaller. We'll try (B) next. If 6 is the smaller of the 2 numbers, then the two numbers are 6 and 7, which have a sum of 13! (B) is the right answer.

If (B) gave us a sum that was still larger than 13, we would have known that (A) was correct. If we had started with answer (C) and it gave us a sum that was less than 13, our next step would have been to try answer (D).

Here's another more challenging example:

Example

Four consecutive multiples of 5 have a sum of 90. What is the greatest of these four numbers?

(A) 10
(B) 15
(C) 20
(D) 30
(E) 40

Start with answer (C). If 20 is the greatest of the four numbers, we need to find the next three multiples of 5 that are smaller than 20. These are 15, 10, and 5, so our four numbers would be 20, 15, 10, and 5. However, the sum of these four numbers is $20 + 15 + 10 + 5 = 50$. The correct numbers must add up to 90, so we know (C) is incorrect.

Because 90 is greater than 50, we know that the greatest of the four numbers must be larger than 20. Therefore, we'll try answer (D) next. If 30 is the greatest of the four numbers, then the numbers are 30, 25, 20, and 15. The sum of these four numbers is $30 + 25 + 20 + 15 = 90$. (D) is correct.

If (D) gave us a sum that was less than 90, we would have known that (E) was the correct answer. If answer (C) gave us a sum that was greater than 90, we would have then tried answer (B).

Math Review

Chapter 4

Introduction

The following review covers all of the math concepts commonly tested on the Middle and Upper Levels of the SSAT, including arithmetic, algebra, geometry, and data interpretation. Remember that the concepts tested at each level of the SSAT span a wide range of grade levels, so you may see content that you haven't learned yet in school. Work through the material appropriate to your grade level. Review the topics you are familiar with first before moving onto topics that are unfamiliar.

Each section is followed by review questions. Practice answering questions quickly and accurately, and spend extra time reviewing concepts that you find difficult. Make flashcards for information that you need to memorize and drill yourself on this information frequently.

Arithmetic

Numbers and Operations

Look over the definitions of the number properties in the table below. In this Section, we will explore what these definitions mean and how to use them.

Number Properties		
Word	Definition	Examples
Integer	Any negative or positive whole number	−3, 0, 5, 400
Positive	Greater than zero	2, 7, 23, 400
Negative	Less than zero	−2, −7, −23, −400
Even	Divisible by two	4, 18, 2002, 0
Odd	Not evenly divisible by two	3, 7, 15, 2001
Factor	An integer that evenly divides into a number	3 and 4 are factors of 12.
Multiple	The result of multiplying a number by an integer	36 and 48 are multiples of 12.
Prime	Only divisible by itself and 1	3, 5, 7, 11, 19, 23
Composite	Divisible by numbers other than itself and 1	4, 12, 15, 20, 21
Consecutive	Whole numbers that follow each other in order with no gaps	2, 3, 4, 5, 6 ...

Integers

An **integer** is any positive or negative whole number. Fractions and decimals are not integers. **Zero** is an integer, but is neither positive nor negative.

Operations

An **operation** is a fancy name for a process that changes one number into another. The most common operations are addition, subtraction, multiplication, and division. Know the following vocabulary related to operations:

Operations		
Word	Definition	Examples
Sum	The result of adding numbers	The sum of 3 and 4 is 7.
Difference	The result of subtracting numbers	The difference between 5 and 2 is 3.
Product	The result of multiplying numbers	The product of 6 and 4 is 24.
Quotient	The result of dividing numbers	The quotient of 40 divided by 5 is 8.
Remainder	The amount left over when a number cannot be evenly divided by another number	When 11 is divided by 2, the result is 5 with a remainder of 1.

Calculators are not permitted on the SSAT. As a result, you will need to be able to solve arithmetic calculations quickly and accurately on paper. In order to make sure that you have mastered all of the basics of long addition, subtraction, multiplication, and division, look through the review below and try the drills that follow.

Addition

To add large numbers, break up the question into parts based on the **place** of the digits. Each digit in a number has a place value, as shown in the following chart. For a more complete chart including place values with decimals, see Section 5.

thousands	hundreds	tens	ones
5	4	1	2

For the number 5,412 above, 5 is in the thousands place, 4 is in the hundreds place, 1 is in the tens place, and 2 is in the ones place.

Use your knowledge of place values to add large numbers by hand. For example, if you had the question:

Example

$$32 + 14$$

First add the ones place digits together, and then add the tens place digits together. 2 and 4 are both in the ones place, and $2 + 4 = 6$. 3 and 1 are both in the tens place, and $3 + 1 = 4$. Therefore, your answer will be:

$$\begin{array}{r} 32 \\ + 14 \\ \hline 46 \end{array}$$

Always start from the rightmost column and move to the left when you are adding.

Recall that sometimes you will need to use **carrying** in addition problems. For example, look at the following problem:

Example

$$45 + 17$$

Your ones place digits are going to add up to a double-digit number: $5 + 7 = 12$.

If you have a double digit number when you add two numbers together in a column, you will need to use carrying. In this case, you will take the ones digit from 12, which is 2, and place it under the ones digit column. Then you will "carry" the tens digit, which is 1, over the top of the tens digit column.

$$\begin{array}{r} 1 \\ 45 \\ + 17 \\ \hline 2 \end{array}$$

Finally, you will add together all of the digits in the tens column, including the 1 that you carried over. $1 + 4 + 1 = 6$, so your answer will be:

$$\begin{array}{r} 1 \\ 45 \\ + 17 \\ \hline 62 \end{array}$$

If you are adding together larger numbers, you may have to carry multiple times. For example:

$$
\begin{array}{r}
\textit{11} \\
7658 \\
+\ 1571 \\
\hline
9229
\end{array}
$$

Subtraction

In subtraction, just like in addition, focus on the place of the digits. Start subtracting the digits in the ones place and then move to the left. For example, if you had the question:

Example
$85 - 23$

You would start by subtracting the ones place digits, which are 5 and 3, and then subtract the tens place digits, which are 8 and 2. $5 - 3 = 2$ and $8 - 2 = 6$. Therefore, your answer will be:

$$
\begin{array}{r}
85 \\
-\ 23 \\
\hline
62
\end{array}
$$

Sometimes in subtraction problems, the digits in your first number will be smaller than the digits in your second number. For example:

Example
$34 - 18$

As you can see, in our ones place column, 4 is smaller than 8. Therefore, you will need to use **borrowing.** You will need to "borrow" from the tens place digit in order to continue with your subtraction.

34 is the same thing as 3 tens and 4 ones. We can borrow from the 3 tens in order to make our ones place larger than 8. To do this, take one of the 3 tens and add it to the 4 ones, turning the 3 tens into 2 tens and the 4 ones into 14:

$$
\begin{array}{r}
\textit{2 14} \\
\cancel{3}\cancel{4} \\
-\ 1\ 8 \\
\hline
\end{array}
$$

14 is larger than 8, so we can subtract the digits in our ones and tens columns as usual. $14 - 8 = 6$ and $2 - 1 = 1$, so:

$$
\begin{array}{r}
2\ 14 \\
\cancel{3\ 4} \\
-\ 1\ 8 \\
\hline
1\ 6
\end{array}
$$

Some problems will require you to borrow multiple times. For example:

$$8762 - 3914$$

We can solve this problem step-by-step, starting with the ones place column and moving to the left.

Our first number has a ones place digit that is smaller than the ones place digit of our second number. As a result, we will need to borrow from the 6 tens in the tens place:

$$
\begin{array}{r}
5\ 12 \\
8\ 7\ \cancel{6}\ \cancel{2} \\
-\ 3\ 9\ 1\ 4 \\
\hline
4\ 8
\end{array}
$$

In our hundreds place, our first number is also smaller than our second number, so we will need to borrow from the 8 in our thousands place. After we have subtracted all of the columns, we can come up with our final answer:

$$
\begin{array}{r}
7\ 17 \\
\cancel{8}\ \cancel{7}\ 6\ 2 \\
-\ 3\ 9\ 1\ 4 \\
\hline
4\ 8\ 4\ 8
\end{array}
$$

Multiplication

You should be very comfortable multiplying whole numbers from 1 to 12 in your head. If you have trouble remembering your **multiplication table**, put this information on flashcards and quiz yourself regularly.

Multiplication Table												
	1	2	3	4	5	6	7	8	9	10	11	12
1	1	2	3	4	5	6	7	8	9	10	11	12
2	2	4	6	8	10	12	14	16	18	20	22	24
3	3	6	9	12	15	18	21	24	27	30	33	36
4	4	8	12	16	20	24	28	32	36	40	44	48
5	5	10	15	20	25	30	35	40	45	50	55	60
6	6	12	18	24	30	36	42	48	54	60	66	72
7	7	14	21	28	35	42	49	56	63	70	77	84
8	8	16	24	32	40	48	56	64	72	80	88	96
9	9	18	27	36	45	54	63	72	81	90	99	108
10	10	20	30	40	50	60	70	80	90	100	110	120
11	11	22	33	44	55	66	77	88	99	110	121	132
12	12	24	36	48	60	72	84	96	108	120	132	144

To solve multiplication problems with larger numbers, rely on your knowledge of the multiplication table for smaller numbers. For example, let's look at this problem:

Example

$$17 \times 6$$

Even though you probably do not have your 17 times tables memorized, you can still easily solve this problem by breaking it down into parts. In this problem, take the number 6 and multiply it first by the ones place, and then by the tens place of the larger number (17).

First, multiply 6 by 7, which is the number in the ones place. Recall from your multiplication table that $6 \times 7 = 42$. Since 42 is a two-digit number, we will need to carry the 4:

$$
\begin{array}{r}
4 \\
17 \\
\times\ 6 \\
\hline
2
\end{array}
$$

Then, we will multiply 6 by 1, which is the number in the tens place. Afterwards, we will add 4, the number that we carried. $6 \times 1 + 4 = 10$, so our final answer will be:

$$
\begin{array}{r}
4 \\
17 \\
\times\ 6 \\
\hline
102
\end{array}
$$

Now take a look at a slightly more complicated problem:

Example

$$45 \times 13$$

In this problem, our second number has two digits. We will need to go through the multiplication process for each digit separately. Let's start with the ones digit, which is 3, and ignore the tens digit for now.

Just like we did in our first example, we'll multiply 3 first by the ones place, followed by the tens place. 5 is the number in the ones place, and $3 \times 5 = 15$. Since we have a two-digit number, we will need to carry the 1. We'll then multiply by 4, which is the number in the tens place, and add the number we carried. $3 \times 4 + 1 = 13$, so we get:

$$
\begin{array}{r}
1 \\
45 \\
\times\ 13 \\
\hline
135
\end{array}
$$

But we're not done yet! Now that we have finished with the "3" in "13", we need to work on the "1." We'll start a new line under the answer. The "1" in 13 is really a "10", because 13 is the same thing as 1 ten plus 3 ones. In order to make our multiplication problem reflect that our "1" is really a "10," we will need to add a zero under our answer:

$$
\begin{array}{r}
45 \\
\times\ 13 \\
\hline
135 \\
0
\end{array}
$$

After we have added the zero, we'll multiply 1 first by the ones place, followed by the tens place. 5 is in the ones place, and $1 \times 5 = 5$. 4 is in the tens place, and $1 \times 4 = 4$. Therefore, we are left with:

$$\begin{array}{r} 45 \\ \times\ 13 \\ \hline 135 \\ 450 \end{array}$$

To get our final answer, we need to add the two lines together:

$$\begin{array}{r} 45 \\ \times\ 13 \\ \hline 135 \\ +\ 450 \\ \hline 585 \end{array}$$

Our final answer is 585.

When you are multiplying even larger numbers, remember to always add another zero when you start a new line. For example:

$$\begin{array}{r} 524 \\ \times\ 212 \\ \hline 1048 \\ 5240 \\ +\ 104800 \\ \hline 111088 \end{array}$$

 Watch Video 1.1, Multiplication, at **videos.ivyglobal.com.**

Division

In order to divide with large numbers, you can also apply your knowledge of the multiplication table.

For example, let's see how we would divide 2406 by 3:

Example

$$3\overline{)2406}$$

To solve this problem, we need to take 3 and divide it into each number, one at a time. Unlike multiplication, however, we're going to work from left to right. 2 is smaller than 3, so 3 cannot divide into 2. As a result, we will move onto the next digit, and try to divide 3 into 24.

3 does divide into 24. Recall from your multiplication tables that $3 \times 8 = 24$. We'll therefore write "8" above "24." To check our work, we'll multiply 3×8 again, and write the product below "24." We'll then subtract to see what remainder we get:

$$
\begin{array}{r}
8 \\
3\overline{)2406} \\
\underline{-24} \\
0
\end{array}
$$

$24 - 24 = 0$, so we'll write "0" as the remainder to finish this step.

In the next step, we'll bring down the next number in 2406, which is 0, and write this next to the remainder from our last step:

$$
\begin{array}{r}
8 \\
3\overline{)2406} \\
\underline{-24} \\
00
\end{array}
$$

Our new number is "00," which is the same thing as 0. We'll then divide 3 into this number. 3 goes into 0 zero times. Following the same process as above, we'll therefore write "0" above the division symbol and multiply by 3 to check our work:

$$
\begin{array}{r}
80 \\
3\overline{)2406} \\
\underline{-24} \\
00 \\
\underline{-0} \\
0
\end{array}
$$

Finally, we'll bring down our last number, which is 6, and we'll divide 3 into this number. Recall that $3 \times 2 = 6$. 3 divides into 6 two times, so we'll write "2" above the division symbol and check whether we have a remainder:

$$
\begin{array}{r}
802 \\
3\overline{)2406} \\
\underline{-24} \\
00 \\
\underline{-0} \\
06 \\
\underline{-6} \\
0
\end{array}
$$

3 divides evenly into 2406, so there is no remainder. Our final answer is 802.

In some cases, your divisor will not divide evenly into your dividend. In such a case, you will be left with a remainder. Let's look at the following example:

$$4 \overline{)6571}$$

Starting with the first number to the left, we see that 4 goes into 6 only once, but not evenly. $4 \times 1 = 4$, and when we subtract 4 from 6, we will have a remainder of 2:

$$
\begin{array}{r}
1 \\
4 \overline{)6571} \\
\underline{-4} \\
2
\end{array}
$$

When we bring down the next number, 5, we'll write this next to the remainder and get a new number, 25. 4 goes into 25 six times because $4 \times 6 = 24$. We'll write "6" above the division symbol. $25 - 24 = 1$, so here we will be left with a remainder of 1:

$$
\begin{array}{r}
16 \\
4 \overline{)6571} \\
\underline{-4} \\
25 \\
\underline{-24} \\
1
\end{array}
$$

Our next step is to bring down the following number, 7, and write this beside our remainder to get 17. 4 goes into 17 four times because $4 \times 4 = 16$. We'll write "4" above the division symbol. $17 - 16 = 1$, so we have a remainder of 1 again:

$$
\begin{array}{r}
164 \\
4 \overline{)6571} \\
\underline{-4} \\
25 \\
\underline{-24} \\
17 \\
\underline{-16} \\
1
\end{array}
$$

Finally, we will bring down the last number, 1, and write this next to our remainder to get 11. 4 goes into 11 two times because $4 \times 2 = 8$. We'll write "2" above the division symbol. $11 - 8 = 2$, so we have a remainder of 3.

Math Review

$$
\begin{array}{r}
1642 \\
4\overline{)6571} \\
\underline{-4} \\
25 \\
\underline{-24} \\
17 \\
\underline{-16} \\
11 \\
\underline{-8} \\
3
\end{array}
$$

Because we have no more numbers to bring down, our final answer is 1,642 with 3 left over. The amount left over is called a **remainder**. We can write this remainder as "R3" above the division line:

$$
\begin{array}{r}
1642 \ R3 \\
4\overline{)6571}
\end{array}
$$

Even and Odd Numbers

Remember that an even number can be evenly divided by 2, and an odd number cannot be evenly divided by 2. This means that an odd number will have a remainder when you try to divide by 2, and an even number will have no remainder.

Here's a fun fact about even and odd numbers: you can predict whether the sum or product of two numbers will be even or odd.

- even + even = even
- odd + odd = even
- odd + even = odd

- even × even = even
- odd × odd = odd
- odd × even = even

Test this on any pair of numbers you can find, and you'll see that it is always true!

Practice Questions: Numbers and Operations

On the next few pages, you'll find several sets of basic arithmetic drill questions. On the SSAT, it is very important to be able to add, subtract, multiply, and divide short and long numbers quickly and accurately by hand. Try to complete these drills as quickly as you can. When you are finished, check your answers.

			Addition Drills			
27 +3	13 +9	39 +2	10 +7	42 +8	75 +6	98 +7
67 +23	72 +35	18 +49	37 +14	68 +41	99 +27	32 +85
55 +12	82 +44	32 +16	63 +14	18 +99	75 +75	69 +64
78 + 98 =	39 + 42 =	18 + 54 =	37 + 84 =	28 + 18 =	90 + 40 =	22 + 53 =
125 +5	534 +9	639 +1	832 +7	422 +9	799 +1	502 +3
648 +22	331 +86	510 +27	396 +19	421 +90	307 +21	517 +17
392 +184	739 +717	402 +184	492 +391	246 +184	582 +909	521 +486
329 428 +186	42 593 +204	821 12 +947	82 194 +53	529 438 +167	625 14 +39	527 941 +368

Subtraction Drills						
13 − 2	62 − 5	41 − 9	73 − 1	64 − 4	94 − 7	40 − 3
72 − 52	81 − 59	54 − 37	90 − 31	84 − 73	29 − 17	40 − 27
99 − 42	58 − 39	56 − 38	84 − 27	91 − 57	30 − 22	73 − 15
86 − 42 =	72 − 65 =	62 − 43 =	95 − 78 =	48 − 43 =	81 − 72 =	57 − 31 =
613 − 5	749 − 7	397 − 9	942 − 3	264 − 4	481 − 9	285 − 7
849 − 31	762 − 40	492 − 32	781 − 39	267 − 69	843 − 85	328 − 57
752 − 321	481 − 278	473 − 327	849 − 212	747 − 381	604 − 518	582 − 175
391 286 − 73	847 41 − 316	904 269 − 79	798 280 − 142	359 90 − 21	740 380 − 242	867 329 − 415

76 +15	34 +76	54 −14	90 −32	86 +55	86 −55	99 −33
67 −31	89 +41	76 −66	54 −31	22 +16	87 −59	33 +99
66 + 42 =	31 − 27 =	54 − 29 =	49 + 96 =	38 + 57 =	27 + 64 =	75 − 35 =
52 − 36 =	96 − 43 =	21 + 68 =	53 + 94 =	92 − 61 =	42 + 53=	49 + 77 =
6 7 +□□ = 8 2	7 2 −□□ = 1 3	3 2 +□□ = 6 4	□□ +6 7 = 9 9	□□ −7 6 = 1 2	3□ −□1 = 2 1	□4 +2□ = 5 5
□4 −3□ = 3 6	6□ +□2 = 8 6	□7 + 3 1 = □0□	□□ −2 3 = 4 7	□9 +3□ = 7 1	□2 −6□ = 8	5 4 +□3 = 7□
341 −142	529 +671	904 −731	641 −232	804 +321	922 −344	798 +421
5 2□ −3□1 = □04	1 4□ +□23 = □08	2□9 −□47 = 1□	□34 + 8□7 = □75□	□□4 +378 = 6 0□	7□7 −□3□ = 2 7 8	□56 +3 4□ = 4 9 7
32 +64 −25	78 −29 +93	65 +31 −19	90 +22 −78	320 −245 +980	975 −629 +528	802 −492 +375

Math Review

Multiplication Drills						
$6 \times 8 =$	$9 \times 6 =$	$3 \times 4 =$	$2 \times 12 =$	$5 \times 9 =$	$3 \times 6 =$	$7 \times 12 =$
$3 \times 7 =$	$6 \times 3 =$	$2 \times 7 =$	$6 \times 0 =$	$8 \times 2 =$	$7 \times 9 =$	$5 \times 4 =$
$9 \times 5 =$	$8 \times 4 =$	$4 \times 7 =$	$12 \times 8 =$	$10 \times 5 =$	$11 \times 3 =$	$6 \times 4 =$
$12 \times 11 =$	$3 \times 9 =$	$4 \times 9 =$	$5 \times 3 =$	$11 \times 9 =$	$2 \times 8 =$	$7 \times 7 =$
$6 \times 2 =$	$12 \times 9 =$	$8 \times 8 =$	$8 \times 7 =$	$12 \times 4 =$	$9 \times 9 =$	$10 \times 6 =$
19 $\times 4$	22 $\times 9$	35 $\times 7$	76 $\times 3$	38 $\times 8$	24 $\times 6$	65 $\times 2$
53 $\times 97$	86 $\times 51$	63 $\times 54$	11 $\times 22$	59 $\times 77$	20 $\times 65$	95 $\times 38$
477 $\times 7$	904 $\times 3$	285 $\times 8$	876 $\times 9$	337 $\times 5$	273 $\times 4$	489 $\times 6$
395 $\times 44$	411 $\times 97$	530 $\times 64$	214 $\times 55$	503 $\times 84$	375 $\times 70$	339 $\times 83$
783 $\times 904$	899 $\times 974$	318 $\times 814$	657 $\times 165$	847 $\times 322$	555 $\times 396$	286 $\times 862$

Division Drills						
8 ÷ 4 =	12 ÷ 6 =	12 ÷ 4 =	12 ÷ 3 =	10 ÷ 2 =	4 ÷ 2 =	18 ÷ 3 =
18 ÷ 6 =	20 ÷ 10 =	15 ÷ 3 =	21 ÷ 7 =	20 ÷ 5 =	16 ÷ 2 =	25 ÷ 5 =
21 ÷ 3 =	30 ÷ 5 =	18 ÷ 2 =	15 ÷ 5 =	24 ÷ 4 =	20 ÷ 4 =	18 ÷ 9 =
35 ÷ 5 =	24 ÷ 6 =	32 ÷ 4 =	42 ÷ 6 =	26 ÷ 2 =	40 ÷ 4 =	24 ÷ 8 =
54 ÷ 9 =	48 ÷ 8 =	42 ÷ 7 =	55 ÷ 5 =	64 ÷ 8 =	36 ÷ 6 =	48 ÷ 6 =
$5\overline{)6}$ R=	$3\overline{)7}$ R=	$4\overline{)9}$ R=	$4\overline{)10}$ R=	$3\overline{)8}$ R=	$2\overline{)9}$ R=	$7\overline{)10}$ R=
$5\overline{)22}$ R=	$3\overline{)20}$ R=	$6\overline{)25}$ R=	$6\overline{)39}$ R=	$8\overline{)67}$ R=	$4\overline{)34}$ R=	$5\overline{)43}$ R=
$5\overline{)435}$	$3\overline{)762}$	$7\overline{)455}$	$8\overline{)392}$	$6\overline{)756}$	$2\overline{)748}$	$9\overline{)711}$
$11\overline{)748}$	$8\overline{)432}$	$3\overline{)297}$	$4\overline{)260}$	$7\overline{)504}$	$5\overline{)785}$	$9\overline{)684}$

Multiplication and Division Drills

$6 \div 3 =$	$6 \times 3 =$	$8 \div 2 =$	$8 \times 2 =$	$36 \div 6 =$	$6 \times 6 =$	$64 \div 8 =$
$10 \div 5 =$	$10 \times 5 =$	$9 \div 3 =$	$9 \times 3 =$	$81 \div 9 =$	$9 \times 9 =$	$7 \times 7 =$
$\begin{array}{r} 56 \\ \times 4 \\ \hline \end{array}$	$\begin{array}{r} 98 \\ \times 6 \\ \hline \end{array}$	$\begin{array}{r} 37 \\ \times 2 \\ \hline \end{array}$	$\begin{array}{r} 86 \\ \times 8 \\ \hline \end{array}$	$\begin{array}{r} 30 \\ \times 3 \\ \hline \end{array}$	$\begin{array}{r} 82 \\ \times 6 \\ \hline \end{array}$	$\begin{array}{r} 39 \\ \times 7 \\ \hline \end{array}$
$5\overline{)785}$	$3\overline{)912}$	$7\overline{)462}$	$8\overline{)400}$	$6\overline{)612}$	$2\overline{)852}$	$9\overline{)1008}$
$5\overline{)34}^{R=}$	$3\overline{)52}^{R=}$	$6\overline{)17}^{R=}$	$6\overline{)45}^{R=}$	$8\overline{)64}^{R=}$	$4\overline{)25}^{R=}$	$5\overline{)52}^{R=}$
$8 \times \square = 40$	$\square \times 7 = 63$	$\square \times 7 = 7$	$\square \times 9 = 0$	$3 \times \square = 27$	$6 \times \square = 48$	$9 \times \square = 36$
$\square \div 7 = 6$	$60 \div \square = 5$	$\square \div 4 = 24$	$\square \div 6 = 24$	$12 \div \square = 4$	$\square \div 9 = 6$	$12 \div \square = 6$
$81 \div \square = 9$	$7 \times \square = 56$	$\square \times 4 = 36$	$\square \times 12 = 36$	$42 \div \square = 6$	$6 \times \square = 18$	$\square \div 5 = 8$
$\begin{array}{r} 744 \\ \times 72 \\ \hline \end{array}$	$\begin{array}{r} 843 \\ \times 21 \\ \hline \end{array}$	$\begin{array}{r} 904 \\ \times 50 \\ \hline \end{array}$	$\begin{array}{r} 371 \\ \times 52 \\ \hline \end{array}$	$\begin{array}{r} 987 \\ \times 47 \\ \hline \end{array}$	$\begin{array}{r} 382 \\ \times 82 \\ \hline \end{array}$	$\begin{array}{r} 426 \\ \times 18 \\ \hline \end{array}$

Section 2
Factors and Multiples

A number is **divisible** by another number if the result of division is a whole number. For instance, 12 is divisible by 3 because $12 \div 3 = 4$ with nothing left over. Because 12 is divisible by 3, we can say that 3 is a **factor** of 12. Because 3 multiplied by a whole number is 12, we can say that 12 is a **multiple** of 3.

Numbers which have a remainder after division are not multiples or factors of each other. For example, 15 is not evenly divisible by 6, because 6 goes into 15 twice with a remainder of 3. Therefore, 6 is not a factor of 15, and 15 is not a multiple of 6.

Finding Factors

When you are trying to find all of the factors of a number, organize them in pairs, starting with 1. Here is how we would find all of the factors of 15:

$$1 \times 15 = 15$$
$$3 \times 5 = 15$$

15 has four factors: 1, 3, 5, and 15.

 Watch Video 1.2, Finding Factors, at **videos.ivyglobal.com.**

Here are some quick ways to test whether one number is divisible by another:

Divisibility Rules		
Divisible by	When	Example
2	The last digit is divisible by 2 (the number is even)	4028 is divisible by 2 because 8 is divisible by 2.
3	The sum of the digits is divisible by 3	465 is divisible by 3 because $4 + 6 + 5 = 15$, which is divisible by 3.
4	The number formed by the last two digits is divisible by 4	340 is divisible by 4 because 40 is divisible by 4.
5	The last digit is 0 or 5	750 is divisible by 5 because it ends in 0.
6	The number is even and the sum of the digits is divisible by 3	1044 is divisible by 6 because it is even and $1 + 0 + 4 + 4 = 9$, which is divisible by 3.
9	The sum of the digits is divisible by 9	1296 is divisible by 9 because $1 + 2 + 9 + 6 = 18$, which is divisible by 9.
10	The last digit is 0	3390 is divisible by 10 because it ends in 0.

 Watch Video 1.3, Divisibility Rules, at **videos.ivyglobal.com**.

Finding Multiples

Any number has an infinite number of multiples, because you can keep multiplying the number by bigger integers to get bigger multiples. Here is how we would find the first three multiples of 12:

$$12 \times 1 = 12$$
$$12 \times 2 = 24$$
$$12 \times 3 = 36$$

The first three multiples of 12 are 12, 24, and 36.

Notice that all numbers are multiples of themselves, because any number multiplied by 1 is itself. All numbers are also factors of themselves, because any number can be divided by itself to give a quotient of 1.

Prime and Composite Numbers

A **prime** number is a number that has only two factors: itself and 1. A prime number is not divisible by any other integers. 1 is not a prime number, because it only has one factor: 1! 2 is the only even prime number. Here is a list of the first ten prime numbers:

- 2, 3, 5, 7, 11, 13, 17, 19, 23, 29...

A **composite** number is a number that has more than two factors. Composite numbers are not prime numbers because they are divisible by three or more integers. For example, 15 is a composite number because it is divisible by 1, 15, 3, and 5.

 Watch Video 1.4, Prime and Composite Numbers, at **videos.ivyglobal.com.**

Factor Trees and Prime Factors

Draw a **factor tree** to find the prime factors of any integer. Start with any two factors of that integer. Then, find two factors of each of these numbers. Continue drawing branches until you end up with only prime numbers at the end of your tree. These are your **prime factors.**

For example, we can draw a factor tree for 72 by starting with the factors 8 and 9:

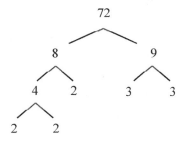

Based on this tree, we see that 72 is the product of the prime factors 2, 2, 2, 3, and 3. We can test this out by multiplying these prime factors together: $2 \times 2 \times 2 \times 3 \times 3 = 72$.

 Watch Video 1.5, Factor Trees, at **videos.ivyglobal.com.**

Greatest Common Factor (GCF)

The **greatest common factor (GCF)** of two integers is the largest integer that is a factor of both integers. For example, 8 is the GCF of 16 and 24. To find the GCF of two numbers, first find their prime factors using factor trees:

Based on these prime factors, we can see that 16 and 24 share three 2s. Multiply these shared prime factors together to find their GCF: $2 \times 2 \times 2 = 8$.

 Watch Video 1.6, Greatest Common Factor, at **videos.ivyglobal.com.**

Least Common Multiple (LCM)

The **least common multiple (LCM)** of two integers is the smallest integer that is a multiple of both integers. For example, 48 is the LCM of 16 and 24. To find the LCM of two numbers, start by creating factor trees. Then, multiply all the numbers in both factor trees excluding any that are repeated.

For instance, we can show the prime factors of 16 and 24 in a Venn Diagram:

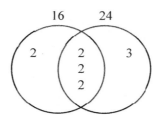

In total, four 2s and one 3 appear in these prime factors, excluding repeats. Therefore, the LCM of 16 and 24 is $2 \times 2 \times 2 \times 2 \times 3 = 48$.

 Watch Video 1.7, Least Common Multiple, at **videos.ivyglobal.com.**

Practice Questions: Factors and Multiples

1. List the first 4 multiples of 2:

2. List the first 5 multiples of 7:

3. List all of the factors of 10:

4. List all of the factors of 48:

5. List all of the prime numbers between 10 and 20:

6. Is 216 divisible by 4?

7. Is 3972 divisible by 3?

8. Is 3972 divisible by 9?

9. Is 123456789 divisible by 6?

10. What is the remainder when 5 is divided by 2?

11. What is the remainder when 35 is divided by 3?

12. What is the remainder when 7 is divided by 7?

13. List all of the prime factors of 18:

14. List all of the prime factors of 34:

15. List all of the prime factors of 84:

16. Find the greatest common factor of 36 and 45:

17. Find the greatest common factor of 1 and 2:

18. Find the least common multiple of 10 and 6:

19. Find the least common multiple of 15 and 5:

20. Let ✿x represent the number of distinct factors of any number x. For example, ✿6 = 4 because 6 has four distinct factors: 1, 2, 3 and 6. What is ✿9?

Fractions

A fraction can be thought of in two ways. Firstly, we can think of fractions as an alternate way of representing division. When we write $\frac{3}{4}$, we mean 3 divided by 4. Because fractions can represent division, we can write any whole number as a fraction! For example, to write the number 2, we could write $\frac{2}{1}$, (2 divided by 1), $\frac{4}{2}$, (4 divided by 2), $\frac{6}{3}$, (6 divided by 3), and so on. Anything divided by itself is 1, so we can write 1 as $\frac{2}{2}, \frac{3}{3}, \frac{4}{4}$, etc.

More generally, fractions represent a portion of a whole. The number on top is called the numerator, which represents the part. The number on the bottom is called the denominator, which represents the whole. In the fraction $\frac{3}{4}$, 3 is the numerator and 4 is the denominator. This fraction means that our whole has been divided into 4 equal pieces, and we are selecting 3 of them.

$$\frac{\text{part}}{\text{whole}} = \frac{\text{numerator}}{\text{denominator}}$$

Equivalent Fractions and Reducing Fractions

Equivalent fractions have exactly the same value, but are written in different ways. For example, we can write one half as $\frac{1}{2}$, which represents one out of two pieces. We can also write it as $\frac{2}{4}$, which represents two out of four pieces, and $\frac{3}{6}$, which represents three out of six pieces. To find equivalent fractions, multiply both the numerator and the denominator by the same number:

$$\frac{1}{2} = \frac{1 \times 2}{2 \times 2} = \frac{2}{4}$$

Reducing fractions means doing this process backwards. When your numerator and denominator share a common factor, reduce your fraction by dividing the top and bottom by this number:

$$\frac{2}{4} = \frac{2 \div 2}{4 \div 2} = \frac{1}{2}$$

A fraction is reduced to its **lowest terms** when the numerator and denominator no longer share any common factors—when you have the smallest possible denominator. In the example above, $\frac{1}{2}$ is in lowest terms because there is no number that divides into both 1 and 2.

 Watch Video 1.8, Intro to Fractions, at **videos.ivyglobal.com.**

Comparing Fractions

When fractions have the **same numerator**, they can be placed in order from least to greatest by ordering their denominators from greatest to least. Or, to put them in order from greatest to least, order the denominators from least to greatest.

Example

Order the following fractions form least to greatest:

$$\frac{6}{2}, \frac{6}{7}, \frac{6}{1}, \frac{6}{3}$$

All of these fractions have the same numerator, 6. To order them from least to greatest, put the fractions in the order where the denominators are ordered from greatest to least. The result is $\frac{6}{7}, \frac{6}{3}, \frac{6}{2}, \frac{6}{1}$.

When fractions have the **same denominator**, you can determine their order from least to greatest by ordering their numerators from least to greatest. Or, to put them in order from greatest to least, order the numerators from greatest to least.

Example

Order the following fractions form least to greatest:

$$\frac{7}{15}, \frac{3}{15}, \frac{12}{15}, \frac{8}{15}$$

All of these fractions have the same denominator, 15. To order them from least to greatest, put the fractions in the order where the numerators are ordered from least to greatest. The result is $\frac{3}{15}, \frac{7}{15}, \frac{8}{15}, \frac{12}{15}$.

To compare fractions that do not have the same numerator or denominator, you first need to convert them into equivalent fractions with the same denominator. Once the fractions have the same denominator, your smallest fraction will have the smallest numerator, and your largest fraction will have the largest numerator.

For example, to compare the fractions $\frac{5}{6}$ and $\frac{7}{9}$, find a common denominator of the two fractions. The easiest way to find a common denominator is to use the least common multiple of both denominators. The least common multiple of 6 and 9 is 18, so we will convert both of these fractions into equivalent fractions with a denominator of 18:

$$\frac{5}{6} = \frac{5 \times 3}{6 \times 3} = \frac{15}{18}$$

$$\frac{7}{9} = \frac{7 \times 2}{9 \times 2} = \frac{14}{18}$$

15 is bigger than 14, so we can see that $\frac{5}{6}$ is bigger than $\frac{7}{9}$.

 Watch Video 1.9, Comparing Fractions, at **videos.ivyglobal.com.**

Adding and Subtracting Fractions

You can only add or subtract two fractions when they have the same denominator. To add or subtract two fractions with different denominators, you first need to convert them to equivalent fractions with the same denominator. Then, you can add or subtract the numerators. For example:

Example

$$\frac{3}{4} + \frac{2}{3}$$

To add $\frac{3}{4}$ and $\frac{2}{3}$, we need to find the least common denominator of both fractions. In this case, 12 is the least common denominator. Then, we need to rewrite these fractions with 12 as the denominator:

$$\frac{3}{4} = \frac{3 \times 3}{4 \times 3} = \frac{9}{12}$$

$$\frac{2}{3} = \frac{2 \times 4}{3 \times 4} = \frac{8}{12}$$

Now that both fractions have the same denominator, we can add them by adding their numerators:

$$\frac{3}{4} + \frac{2}{3} = \frac{9}{12} + \frac{8}{12} = \frac{17}{12}$$

If we wanted to subtract these fractions, we would go through the same process and then subtract the numerators:

$$\frac{3}{4} - \frac{2}{3} = \frac{9}{12} - \frac{8}{12} = \frac{1}{12}$$

Watch Video 1.10, Adding and Subtracting Fractions, at **videos.ivyglobal.com.**

Mixed Numbers and Improper Fractions

A **mixed number** is a combination of a whole number and a fraction. For instance, $1\frac{2}{5}$ is a mixed number that means "1 and 2 fifths," or "1 plus 2 fifths." To add or subtract mixed numbers, we must convert them to **improper fractions**, which are fractions where the numerator is bigger than the denominator. Here's how:

- First, write your mixed number as an addition problem: $1\frac{2}{5} = 1 + \frac{2}{5}$

- Then, convert your whole number into a fraction with the same denominator. 1 is the same as 5 fifths, so we can write: $1 + \frac{2}{5} = \frac{5}{5} + \frac{2}{5}$

- Then, add the two fractions by adding their numerators: $\frac{5}{2} + \frac{2}{5} = \frac{7}{5}$. This improper fraction means the same thing as the mixed number $1\frac{2}{5}$.

To go backwards and convert an improper fraction into a mixed number, you need to remember that a fraction can also mean division. Divide the numerator by the denominator to get a whole number and a remainder. This remainder becomes the numerator of your new fraction.

For example, $\frac{13}{6}$ means 13 divided by 6, which is 2 with a remainder of 1. Therefore, we would write the mixed number as $2\frac{1}{6}$.

Watch Video 1.11, Mixed Numbers and Improper Fractions, at **videos.ivyglobal.com.**

Multiplying and Dividing Fractions

Multiplying fractions is very easy. Simply multiply the numerators and the denominators:

$$\frac{4}{5} \times \frac{3}{7} = \frac{4 \times 3}{5 \times 7} = \frac{12}{35}$$

 Watch Video 1.12, Multiplying Fractions, at **videos.ivyglobal.com.**

To divide one fraction by another, multiply the first fraction (the dividend) by the reciprocal of the second fraction (the divisor). **Reciprocal** is just a fancy word for the upside-down version of a fraction. After flipping the second fraction upside-down, multiply straight across:

$$\frac{4}{5} \div \frac{3}{7} = \frac{4}{5} \times \frac{7}{3} = \frac{4 \times 7}{5 \times 3} = \frac{28}{15}$$

 Watch Video 1.13, Dividing Fractions, at **videos.ivyglobal.com.**

Practice Questions: Fractions

1. Reduce $\frac{16}{48}$ to lowest terms:

2. Reduce $\frac{12}{32}$ to lowest terms:

3. Re-write $\frac{3}{4}$ with a denominator of 12:

4. Re-write $\frac{3}{5}$ with a denominator of 25:

For questions 5-8, put the fractions in order from greatest to least:

5. $\frac{9}{7}, \frac{4}{7}, \frac{1}{7}, \frac{12}{7}$

6. $\frac{5}{2}, \frac{5}{8}, \frac{5}{3}, \frac{5}{6}$

7. $\frac{12}{8}, \frac{4}{8}, \frac{1}{8}, \frac{10}{8}$

8. $\frac{3}{8}, \frac{3}{2}, \frac{3}{3}, \frac{3}{7}$

9. Which is bigger, $\frac{4}{7}$ or $\frac{7}{10}$?

10. Which is bigger, $\frac{3}{5}$ or $\frac{5}{9}$?

11. $\dfrac{2}{3} + \dfrac{4}{5} =$

12. $\dfrac{2}{5} + \dfrac{4}{3} =$

13. $\dfrac{4}{5} - \dfrac{1}{2} =$

14. $\dfrac{8}{9} - \dfrac{3}{4} =$

15. $1\dfrac{5}{6} + \dfrac{1}{12} =$

16. Write $1\dfrac{2}{3}$ as an improper fraction:

17. Write $3\dfrac{1}{7}$ as an improper fraction:

18. Write $\dfrac{10}{3}$ as a mixed number:

19. Write $\dfrac{9}{5}$ as a mixed number:

20. $\dfrac{3}{8} \times \dfrac{1}{4} =$

21. $\dfrac{5}{8} \div \dfrac{2}{3} =$

22. $\dfrac{3}{4} \times 5 =$

23. $1\dfrac{3}{5} \times \dfrac{1}{2} =$

24. $4\dfrac{6}{7} \div 2 =$

Section 4
Ratios

While a fraction represents a relationship between a part and a whole, a **ratio** represents a relationship between two or more parts. For instance, a ratio might compare the number of girls to the number of boys in a class, or the amount of sugar to the amount of water in a recipe. A ratio can be expressed using words, a colon, or a numerator and a denominator like a fraction:

- The ratio of boys to girls is 2 to 3.
- The ratio of boys to girls is 2:3.
- The ratio of boys to girls is $\frac{2}{3}$.

All of these ways of writing ratios mean the same thing: for every 2 boys in the class, there are 3 girls.

Converting Between Ratios and Fractions

You will sometimes be asked to convert between ratios and fractions. Remember that the two numbers in a ratio are both parts, while the denominator in a fraction represents the whole. Therefore, you need to add both parts together to find your new denominator. For example:

Example

The ratio of boys to girls in a class is $\frac{2}{3}$. If there are 12 girls in the class, what is the fraction of boys in the class?

You can write this as an equation. If the ratio of boys to girls in the class is $\frac{2}{3}$, the fraction of boys in the class is $\frac{2}{2+3} = \frac{2}{5}$. The fraction of girls in the class is $\frac{3}{2+3} = \frac{3}{5}$.

Word Problems with Ratios

You may need to use your knowledge of equivalent fractions to solve word problems involving ratios. For example:

Example

The ratio of boys to girls in a class is $\frac{2}{3}$. If there are 12 girls in the class, what is the number of boys in the class?

You can write this as an equation:

$$\frac{\text{boys}}{\text{girls}} = \frac{2}{3} = \frac{?}{12}$$

This equation is asking you to re-write the ratio $\frac{2}{3}$ with a denominator of 12. To do this, multiply both the numerator and the denominator by the same number to find the equivalent ratio:

$$\frac{\text{boys}}{\text{girls}} = \frac{2 \times 4}{3 \times 4} = \frac{8}{12}$$

If the ratio of boys to girls is $\frac{2}{3}$ and there are 12 girls in the class, there must be 8 boys in the class.

 Watch Video 1.14, Intro to Ratios, at **videos.ivyglobal.com.**

Cross-Multiplying: Upper Level Only

In examples like the one above where two ratios are set equal to each other, you can also solve for the missing variable by **cross-multiplying**:

$$\text{If } \frac{a}{b} = \frac{c}{d}, \text{ then } ad = cb$$

Example

A recipe calls for a ratio of 2 teaspoons of cinnamon for every 3 teaspoons of sugar. If you want to use 7 teaspoons of cinnamon, how much sugar do you need?

First, set up an equation and let x represent the amount of sugar:

$$\frac{2}{3} = \frac{7}{x}$$

Then, cross-multiply and solve:

$$2x = 21$$

$$x = 10.5$$

For 7 teaspoons of cinnamon, you need 10.5 teaspoons of sugar.

 Watch Video 1.15, Cross Multiplying, at **videos.ivyglobal.com.**

(See sections under Algebra for more information about solving algebraic equations.)

Practice Questions: Ratios

For questions 1-4, consider the following information: A class library has 200 books, of which 20 are history books and 30 are math books.

1. What is the ratio of history books to math books?

2. What is the ratio of history books to non-history books?

3. What fraction of the library's books are math books?

4. If the library adds 50 new books, what would be the ratio of new books to old books?

5. Jenny bought a bag of gummy worms and hard candies. In the bag, the ratio of gummy worms to hard candies is 3 to 5. What is the fraction of hard candies in the bag?

6. A school has a student-teacher ratio of 15 to 1. If the school has 22 teachers, how many students are at the school?

7. A recipe says to add a ratio of 3 cups of water to every 2 cups of rice. If John adds 6 cups of rice, how much water should he add?

For questions 8-11, consider the following information: Mrs. Markle has a jar of green, red, and blue marbles on her desk. In the jar, the ratio of green to red to blue marbles is 3:2:4.

8. What is the ratio of green marbles to non-green marbles?

9. What is the fraction of blue marbles in the jar?

10. If there are 12 red marbles, how many green marbles are in the jar?

11. If there are 12 red marbles, how many total marbles are in the jar?

12. If 12 inches are equivalent to 30.48 centimeters, and there are 36 inches in one yard, how many centimeters are equivalent to one yard?

13. A store sells flour in 1-pound bags, which cost $1.50, and 5-pound bags, which cost $3.50. If Dominique needs to buy 10 pounds of flour, how much money will she save by buying 5-pound bags instead of 1-pound bags?

14. Monica has a wooden board 27 centimeters long. She needs to cut the board into two pieces whose lengths are in a ratio of 4:5. How long should she make the smallest piece?

15. The instructions for Kevin's plant fertilizer said to dissolve 1 packet of fertilizer in 2.5 cups of water. If Kevin is using 6 cups of water, how many packets of fertilizer does he need?

Questions 16-18 is Upper Level Only.

16. Amy can read 10 pages of her textbook in 15 minutes. How many pages can she read in 40 minutes?

17. If a fruit stand sells 5 kilograms of apples for $6.75, how many kilograms of apples can Carlos buy for $2.70?

18. The tax on a car valued at $30,000 is $1,200. If there is a $2,000 tax on a second car and the same tax rate applies, what is the value of the second car?

Section 5
Decimals

Decimals are another way of writing fractions without using a numerator or a denominator. In the decimal system, digits to the right of the decimal point represent fractions with a denominator of 10, 100, 1000, and so on. These digits fall into the tenths, hundredths, and thousandths place values. For instance, the number 351.748 could be read as "three hundred and fifty-one, and seven tenths, four hundredths, and eight thousandths" based on the place values of its digits:

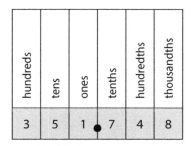

You would arrive at this number by adding the following fractions:

$$351.748 = 300 + 50 + 1 + \frac{7}{10} + \frac{4}{100} + \frac{8}{1000}$$

Adding and Subtracting Decimals

To add or subtract numbers with decimals, make sure you line up the decimal point:

$$
\begin{array}{r}
8.51 \\
+\ 17.34 \\
\hline
25.85
\end{array}
\qquad\qquad
\begin{array}{r}
10.25 \\
-\ 2.11 \\
\hline
8.14
\end{array}
$$

 Watch Video 1.16, Intro to Decimals, at **videos.ivyglobal.com.**

Multiplying and Dividing Decimals

To multiply decimals, it doesn't matter whether your decimal points are lined up. Line up your two numbers in the most convenient way, and multiply as normal. Then, count the number of total digits to the right of the decimal point in both numbers, and move over the decimal point in your answer this many spaces:

$$
\begin{array}{r} 1.52 \\ \times\ 0.4 \\ \hline 0.608 \end{array}
\qquad\qquad
\begin{array}{r} 50 \\ \times\ 0.11 \\ \hline 05.50 \end{array}
$$

To divide decimals, you want to make sure that the number outside of the long division symbol, the divisor, is an integer. To do this, move the decimal point over the same number of spaces for both numbers and divide as usual. It is okay if you still have a decimal point in the number underneath the long division symbol. Re-write this decimal point in exactly the same position on top of the long division symbol, where you will put your answer:

$$
0.2\overline{)3.432} \quad = \quad 2\overline{)34.32} \;(17.16)
$$

If you run out of spaces to move your decimal point in the number underneath the long division symbol, just add an appropriate number of zeros:

$$
3.25\overline{)13.00} \quad = \quad 325\overline{)1300} \;(4)
$$

Watch Video 1.17, Multiplying and Dividing Decimals, at **videos.ivyglobal.com.**

Rounding Decimals

Rounding is a method we use to simplify a number. It is useful when we are trying to estimate, or make a rough calculation. We can round a number to any place value that is convenient, such as the nearest tenth, hundredth, or hundred.

To round a number to any place value, circle the number in that place value. Then, look at the digit directly to the right of this circled number.

- If the digit to the right is less than 5, keep the circled number the same and change all digits to the right of this number to zero.
- If the digit to the right is equal to or greater than 5, add 1 to the circled number and change all digits to the right of this number to zero.

Round 5412.798 to the nearest hundred.

First, locate the number in the hundreds place and circle it. This is the number 4. Then, look at the digit directly to its right, which is the digit 1. 1 is less than 5, so keep 4 the same and change all numbers to its right to zero. The answer is 5400.000.

Round 2318.76 to the nearest tenth.

First, locate the number in the tenths place and circle it. This is the number 7. Then, look at the digit directly to its right, which is the digit 6. Because 6 is greater than 5, we are going to add 1 to our circled number, 7:

$$7 + 1 = 8$$

All of the numbers to the right of this number will be changed to zero. The answer is 2318.80.

In order to estimate or simplify an arithmetic problem, we can round all of the numbers and then perform the operation on the simplified numbers. The answer should be a good estimate of the real answer.

For example, to add 23 to 56, you can round each number to the nearest ten. $20 + 60 = 80$ is a simpler problem. The real answer is 79, so our estimate is close.

Converting Between Fractions and Decimals

There are two ways to convert from a fraction to a decimal. The short way, which will work for a lot of fractions but not all of them, is to convert your fraction into an equivalent fraction with a denominator of 10, 100, or 1000. Then, re-write this fraction as a decimal:

$$\frac{11}{20} = \frac{11 \times 5}{20 \times 5} = \frac{55}{100} = 0.55$$

The long way, which will work for all fractions, is to treat your fraction as a long division problem and divide your numerator by your denominator:

$$20 \overline{)11.00} = 0.55$$

To convert from a decimal to a fraction, re-write your decimal as a fraction with a denominator of 10, 100, or 1000. Then, reduce into lowest terms:

$$0.68 = \frac{68}{100} = \frac{68 \div 4}{100 \div 4} = \frac{17}{25}$$

 Watch Video 1.18, Converting Between Fractions & Decimals, at **videos.ivyglobal.com.**

Practice Questions: Decimals

1. $1.25 + 4.75 =$

2. $3.65 + 4.7 =$

3. $7.4 - 1.02 =$

4. $15.42 + 0.675 =$

5. $3.78 - 2.5 =$

6. $5.36 - 0.005 =$

7. $4 \times 6.7 =$

8. $115.5 \times 0.4 =$

9. $8 \div 1.6 =$

10. $0.8 \div 16 =$

11. $8.68 \times 3.3 =$

12. $4.2 \div 0.7 =$

13. $15.96 \div 3.8 =$

For questions 14-16, round each number to the nearest tenth:

14. 29.061

15. 3189.5204

16. 40.976

For questions 17-19, round each number to the nearest thousand:

17. 58421.3

18. 75002

19. 948.42

20. Write $\dfrac{7}{8}$ as a decimal:

21. Write $\dfrac{9}{50}$ as a decimal:

22. Write $\dfrac{3}{25}$ as a decimal:

23. Write $\dfrac{19}{40}$ as a decimal:

24. Write 0.25 as a fraction:

25. Write 0.6 as a fraction:

26. Write 0.35 as a fraction:

Section 6
Percents

A **percent** is another way of expressing a fraction with a denominator of 100. The word "percent" means "out of 100." For example, 30% means "30 out of 100."

Converting Among Percents, Fractions and Decimals

A percent can always be re-written as a fraction with a denominator of 100. Write your percent as the numerator, 100 as the denominator, and reduce to lowest terms:

$$30\% = \frac{30}{100} = \frac{3}{10}$$

A percent is easily re-written as a decimal. Because your percent represents a certain number of hundredths, write this number in the hundredths place:

$$30\% = 30 \text{ hundredths} = 0.30 \text{ or } 0.3$$

Similarly, it is very simple to convert a decimal into a percent. Just multiply your decimal by 100 (move the decimal point over two places to the right) and add a percent sign:

$$0.45 = 45\%$$

There are two ways to convert a fraction into a percent. The fast way, which will work for some fractions, is to convert your fraction into an equivalent fraction with a denominator of 100. Your numerator then becomes your percent:

$$\frac{11}{20} = \frac{11 \times 5}{20 \times 5} = \frac{55}{100} = 55\%$$

The slower way, which will work for all fractions, is to first convert the fraction into a decimal using long division, and then convert your decimal into a percent:

$$20\overline{)11.00}^{0.55}$$

$$0.55 = 55\%$$

 Watch Video 1.19, Intro to Percents, at **videos.ivyglobal.com.**

Common Equivalences

You should learn the most common equivalent fractions, decimals, and percents, given in the chart below. The horizontal line above a decimal digit means that it repeats indefinitely.

Fraction, Decimal, and Percent Equivalences		
Fraction	Decimal	Percent
$\frac{1}{2}$	0.5	50%
$\frac{1}{4}$	0.25	25%
$\frac{3}{4}$	0.75	75%
$\frac{1}{3}$	$0.\overline{3}$	33.33%
$\frac{2}{3}$	$0.\overline{6}$	66.67%
$\frac{1}{5}$	0.2	20%
$\frac{2}{5}$	0.4	40%
$\frac{3}{5}$	0.6	60%
$\frac{4}{5}$	0.8	80%
$\frac{1}{8}$	0.125	12.5%

Solving Percent Problems: Step 1

In order to solve word problems involving percents, you will need to be very skilled at converting among percents, decimals, and fractions. Be sure you are entirely comfortable with this process before moving on to word problems.

For example, consider the following question:

Example

On his last science test, Adam answered 15 questions correctly and 5 questions incorrectly. He did not leave any questions blank. What percent of the questions did he answer correctly?

There are two ways to solve this question. First, you could write a fraction that represents the number of questions he answered correctly out of the total number of questions on the test, and then convert this fraction into a percent. Because he answered 15 questions correctly and there were 20 questions on the test, you would write:

$$\frac{15}{20} = \frac{15 \times 5}{20 \times 5} = \frac{75}{100} = 75\%$$

Or, you could convert this fraction into a decimal using long division, and then convert that decimal into a percent:

$$20\overline{)15.00}^{\,0.75}$$

$$0.75 = 75\%$$

Either way, you find that Adam answered 75% of the questions correctly.

Solving Percent Problems: Step 2

You may also be asked to find a certain percent of a number. In this case, remember that the word "of" means "multiply." Convert your percent into a fraction or decimal, and then multiply by your given number.

For example, consider the following question:

Example

As a special promotion, all clothes at a certain boutique are now discounted 40%. If the regular price of a dress at this boutique is $80, what is the discounted price?

You can find 40% of $80 in two ways. First, you could convert 40% into a fraction, and then multiply this fraction by $80:

$$40\% = \frac{40}{100} = \frac{40 \div 20}{100 \div 20} = \frac{2}{5}$$

$$\frac{2}{5} \times \$80 = \frac{\$160}{5} = \$32$$

You could also convert 40% into a decimal and then multiply by $80:

$$40\% = \frac{40}{100} = 0.40$$

$$\begin{array}{r} \$80 \\ \times .40 \\ \hline \$32.00 \end{array}$$

You have now found that 40% of $80 is $32. However, the dress is 40% off of the original price, which means that you have to subtract $32 from $80 to find the discounted price:

$$\$80 - \$32 = \$48$$

The discounted price of the dress is $48.

 Watch Video 1.20, Solving Percent Problems, at **videos.ivyglobal.com.**

Solving Percent Problems with Algebra: Upper Level Only

Some percent problems will require you to set up an algebraic equation (see Algebra for more information about solving algebraic equations).

For example, consider the following problem:

Example

A book has been discounted 25%, which means that the discounted price is $3 lower than the original price. What was the original price of the book?

Based on this information, we can write the following sentence:

$3 is 25% of the original price of the book.

Now, we need to put this sentence into an algebraic equation. "Is" means "equals," "of" means "multiply," and we will let x represent the unknown original price of the book:

$$\$3 = 25\% \times x$$

Then, convert 25% into a fraction or decimal, and solve for x:

$$\$3 = 0.25x$$

$$x = \$12$$

The original price of the book was $12.

 Watch Video 1.21, Solving Percent Problems with Algebra, at **videos.ivyglobal.com.**

Practice Questions: Percents

For all questions involving fractions, reduce fractions to lowest terms.

1. Write 60% as a fraction:

2. Write 37% as a decimal:

3. Write 85% as a fraction:

4. Write 29% as a decimal:

5. Write 0.73 as a percent:

6. Write 0.326 as a percent:

7. Write $\dfrac{3}{5}$ as a percent.

8. Write $\dfrac{11}{25}$ as a percent.

9. Write $\dfrac{5}{8}$ as a percent.

10. What is 80% of 45?

11. What is 70% of 90?

12. What is 37% of 300?

13. What is 25% of 60% of 500?

14. Amanda's class has 11 girls and 9 boys. What percent of the class are boys?

15. John has gray, blue, black, and white shirts in his drawer. If he has 4 gray shirts, 3 blue shirts, 6 black shirts, and 7 white shirts, what percent of his shirts are black?

16. Kevin's class has 30 students. If 40% of the students own pets, how many students do not own pets?

17. A CD is on sale for 25% off of the regular price. If the regular price is $16.40, how much is the sale price?

18. Out of all of the jelly beans in a jar, 30% are green. Of the green jelly beans, 75% are lime-flavored. If there are 400 total jelly beans in the jar, how many are lime-flavored?

Questions 19-20 are Upper Level Only.

19. Elise answered 90% of the questions on her math exam correctly. If she answered 2 questions incorrectly and skipped 3 questions, how many total questions were on the exam?

20. In an appliance store, a refrigerator is on sale for 35% off of the original price. If the discounted price is $130, what was the original price?

Section 7
Word Problems

Many questions on the SSAT ask you to solve a word problem with your knowledge of math and logic. We've already discussed many word problems that involve arithmetic, fractions, ratios, decimals, and percents. In this Section, we'll look at a few more concepts that are helpful for solving SSAT word problems.

Time

In math problems involving time, you will be dealing with seconds, minutes, hours, days and weeks. These quantities of time are related to each other as follows:

- There are 60 seconds in a minute.
- There are 60 minutes in an hour.
- There are 24 hours in a day.

The day is divided into 24 hours. These 24 hours are split into two 12-hour periods denoted by AM (morning hours) and PM (night hours). Be sure to pay attention to whether the question states AM or PM! The format used to represent time has a colon separating the hours from minutes with AM or PM following. For example, 12:34 PM represents the time twelve hours and 34 minutes in the afternoon. *Important!* Remember that midnight is 12:00 AM and noon is 12:00 PM.

Remember the following facts about days, weeks, months, and years:

- There are 7 days in a week.
- There are 30 days in the months of April, June, September, and November.
- There are 31 days in the months of January, March, May, July, August, October, and December.
- There are usually 28 days in February, but every four years there is a "leap year" where February has 29 days.
- There are usually 365 days in a year. Can you guess how many days are in a leap year?

Money

When dealing with questions involving amounts of money, it is important to pay attention to the location of the decimal point. Always write your dollar amounts with two digits to the right of the decimal to represent the number of cents. For example, if you wanted to say that you have 5 dollars, you would write it as $5.00, showing two digits to the right of the decimal that represent 0 cents. If you had 5 dollars and 25 cents, it would be written as $5.25. When you are doing addition and subtraction problems involving money, make sure you line up your decimal points so that you don't mix up your place values.

You should be familiar with the following coins and how much they are worth:

Coin	Value
Penny	$0.01
Nickel	$0.05
Dime	$0.10
Quarter	$0.25
Dollar	$1.00

Units

Units are standard quantities of measurement. Seconds, minutes, hours, and days are all units of time. Dollars and cents are units of money. A dozen is a unit that refers to a group of 12 things. Eggs are frequently sold by the dozen—that is, in groups of 12.

There are two systems of units frequently used to measure mass, length, and volume. The **imperial system** is used frequently in the United States. The imperial system measures weight in pounds (abbreviated *lb*), and it uses the following units to measure length:

- Inch
- Foot: 12 inches
- Yard: 3 feet (36 inches)
- Mile: 1,760 yards (5,280 feet, 63,360 inches)

The imperial system uses the following units to measure volume:

- Cup
- Pint: 2 cups
- Quart: 2 pints (4 cups)
- Gallon: 4 quarts (8 pints, 16 cups)

The **metric system** is very important to learn because it is used more commonly internationally and in the scientific community. In the metric system, mass is measured in grams, length is measured in meters, and volume is measured in liters. Each of these units can be abbreviated as *g* for grams, *m* for meters and *l* for liters.

The metric system also has prefixes, or different word beginnings, that indicate different multiples of 10. These prefixes can be combined with any units (grams, meters, or liters) to result in the multiplied amounts:

- Kilo = 1000
- Hecto = 100
- Deca = 10
- Deci = $^1/_{10}$
- Centi = $^1/_{100}$
- Milli = $^1/_{1000}$

For example, a kilometer is 1000 meters, a decaliter is 10 liters, and a milligram is 1/1000 of a gram, or 0.001 grams.

Each prefix also has a short form that is combined with the unit to make writing simpler.

- Kilo: k
- Hecto: h
- Deca: D
- Deci: d
- Centi: c
- Milli: m

Instead of writing "kilogram," we can write the abbreviation "kg." Instead of "millimeter," we can write "mm." Questions on the SSAT may be written in abbreviations, so it is important to know what these mean.

Here's a quick way to remember the correct order of prefixes. If you write out the prefix abbreviations from biggest to smallest, you'll get:

k h D d c m

A common phrase to remember this order is **K**ing **H**enry **D**ied **D**rinking **C**hocolate **M**ilk.

The SSAT may also ask you to convert between different prefixes. As you move up the list of prefixes, the next unit is 10 times greater than the unit below it. As you move down the list, the next unit is one-tenth the unit above it. To move from one prefix to another, set up a ratio between the two units. For example:

How many meters are equal to 16 kilometers?

From our chart on the previous page, we know that one kilometer equals 1,000 meters. To figure out how many meters equal 16 kilometers, we can set up the following ratio:

$$\frac{\text{meters}}{\text{kilometers}} = \frac{1000}{1} = \frac{?}{16}$$

$$\frac{\text{meters}}{\text{kilometers}} = \frac{1000 \times 16}{1 \times 16} = \frac{16,000}{16}$$

Because there are 1,000 meters in 1 kilometer, there must be 16,000 meters in 16 kilometers.

Patterns

SSAT word problems may also involve **patterns**, or lists that follow a rule. This rule tells you what to do to get the next item in the pattern. For example, the counting numbers follow a pattern where you take the first number 1, and you add one to get the second number 2. Then you add one to this number to get the third number 3, and so on.

A pattern involving numbers is called a **sequence**, and the numbers in the pattern are called **terms**. There are two categories of sequences:

- In the first category, a number is *added* to each term to get the next term. For example, if we start with the number 5 and add 2 to get 7, then add 2 to 7 to get 9, and continue adding 2, we get the sequence 5, 7, 9, 11, 13. In this sequence, 5 is the first term, 7 is the second term and 13 is the fifth term of the sequence.
- In the second category, a number is *multiplied* by a term to get the next term. For example, if we start with the number 5 and multiply it by 2 to get 10, and then multiply 10 by 2 to get 20, and keep multiplying by 10, we get the sequence 5, 10, 20, 40, 80.

If you are asked to determine a specific term in a sequence, you must first figure out the rule that is being used. If you have an "adding sequence," look for the constant number that is added to each term to get the next one. This can be found by subtracting any number in the list from the number after it.

How would you find the next number in the list below?

5, 7, 9, 11, 13

To determine the rule in this sequence, we can subtract any two consecutive numbers in the list. For example, we can calculate $9 - 7 = 2$, or $13 - 11 = 2$, or $7 - 5 = 2$. This tells us the rule for this sequence: add 2 to any term in the sequence and you'll find the next term.

Now that we know the rule, we can find the next number in the sequence by adding 2: $13 + 2 = 15$.

The next number in this sequence is 15.

If the list is a "multiplying sequence," look for the constant number that each term is multiplied by. This can be found by dividing any term by the term before it.

Example

What comes next in the sequence below?

$$5, 10, 20, 40, 80$$

To determine the rule in this sequence, we can divide any of the terms by the term before it. For example, we can calculate $40 \div 20 = 2$, or $20 \div 10 = 2$, or $10 \div 5 = 2$. This tells us the rule for this sequence: multiply any term in the sequence by 2 and you'll find the next term. Now that we know the rule, we can find the next number in the sequence by multiplying the last number by 2:

$$80 \times 2 = 160$$

The next number in this sequence is 160.

If you are trying to determine whether a sequence is produced by adding or multiplying, try out both of these methods and see which one works for all of the terms that you are given.

Practice Questions: Word Problems

1. Thomas arrived at the park 18 minutes before noon. His sister arrived at the park 25 minutes later. At what time did his sister arrive at the park?

2. A play started at 8:30 PM and ended at 10:09 PM. How long was the play?

3. It takes two and a half hours to drive to the zoo. If Sam's family wants to arrive at the zoo when it opens at 10:15 AM, at what time should they leave home?

For questions 4-7, write the total dollar and cent amount for the following combinations of coins:

4. Four dollars, 8 dimes, 3 nickels, 8 pennies

5. 8 dollars, 9 quarters, 6 dimes, 7 nickels, 2 pennies

6. 7 quarters, 6 nickels, 8 pennies

7. One $20 bill, 6 dollars, 8 quarters, 5 dimes, 5 pennies

For questions 8-11, write a combination of coins that would equal the following totals:

8. $0.45

9. $2.64

10. $1.03

11. $3.57

12. After spending $15.92 on a skateboard, Joe has $2.08 left. How much money did Joe have before he bought the skateboard?

13. Corwin has $32.55 to spend on hamburgers. If each hamburger costs $7.00, how many hamburgers can Corwin buy?

14. Raquel divides the money in her piggybank by 3 and adds $7. The result is $15. How much money did Raquel start with?

15. Jean earns $12 per hour. She was paid $444.00 for this week of work. How many hours did she work this week?

16. 25 kilograms is equal to how many grams?

17. 478 milliliters is equal to how many liters?

18. Cleo measured a length of string equal to 0.047 km. If she cuts the string into equal pieces that are each 50 cm long, how many pieces will she have?

19. What number comes next in the pattern below?

    37, 41, 45, 49, 53, __

20. What is the missing number in the pattern below?

    64, 32, 16, __, 4,

21. On his first day at school, Tommy made 1 friend. On his second day, he made 3 friends. On his third day, he made 9 friends, and on his fourth day, he made 27 friends. If this pattern continues, how many friends will Tommy make on his fifth day of school?

22. Gita sorted her marbles into bags. She placed 3 marbles in the first bag, 4 marbles in the second bag, 6 marbles in the third bag, and 9 marbles in the fourth bag. If she continued this pattern, how many marbles did she put in the sixth bag?

Section 8
Negative Numbers

Positive numbers are greater than zero. **Negative numbers** are smaller than zero and have a negative sign (–) in front of them. They are found to the left of zero on a number line. Zero itself is neither positive nor negative:

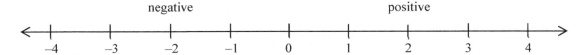

You might ask why negative numbers are useful. It is true that we rarely talk about quantities smaller than zero. However, we frequently use negative numbers when talking about losses, deficits, or decreases in quantities over time. For instance, we could say, "There was a –3° change in temperature between 4pm and 9pm." This means that the temperature dropped 3°. Or, your bank statement for your checking account could read –$50. This means that you have a deficit of $50: you accidentally spent $50 more than you had in your checking account, and you owe money to the bank!

 Watch Video 1.22, Intro to Negative Numbers, at **videos.ivyglobal.com.**

Adding and Subtracting Negative Numbers

It is easiest to visualize addition and subtraction with negative numbers if you use a number line.

To add a positive number, you need to move right a certain number of places on the number line. For instance, if we wanted to add –2 + 5, we would start with –2 on the number line and move 5 places to the right:

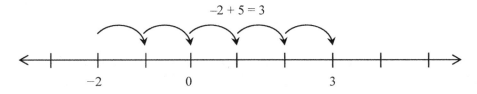

To subtract a positive number, you need to move left a certain number of places on the number line. For instance, if we wanted to subtract −1 − 3, we would start with –1 on the number line and move 3 places to the left:

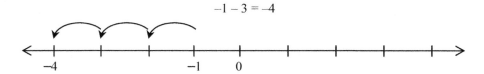

$$-1 - 3 = -4$$

To add a negative number, you actually need to move a certain number of spaces left on the number line—adding a negative number is the same thing as subtracting a positive number! For instance, if we wanted to add 4 + (−2), we would start with 4 on the number line and move 2 spaces to the left:

$$4 + (-2) = 2$$

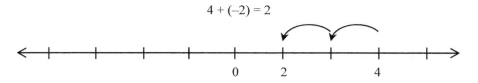

Similarly, to subtract a negative number, you need to move a certain number of spaces right on the number line—subtracting a negative number is the same thing as adding a positive number! For instance, if we wanted to subtract −2 − (−3), we would start with −2 on the number line and move 3 spaces to the right:

$$-2 - (-3) = 1$$

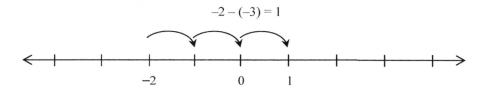

To add or subtract negative numbers without a number line, follow these three rules:

- To add two numbers with the same sign, add the numbers as usual and keep their sign:

$$7 + 13 = 20 \qquad\qquad -7 + (-13) = -20$$

- To add two numbers with different signs, subtract the two numbers and keep the sign of the number that is farthest away from zero:

$$5 + (-4) = +(5 - 4) = 1 \qquad\qquad -6 + 2 = -(6 - 2) = -4$$

- To subtract any two numbers, flip the sign of the second number to its opposite, and then add the two numbers:

$$-4 - 5 = -4 + (-5) = -9 \qquad\qquad 17 - (-4) = 17 + 4 = 21$$

 Watch Video 1.23, Adding and Subtracting Negative Numbers, at **videos.ivyglobal.com.**

Math Review

Multiplying and Dividing Negative Numbers

Multiplying and dividing negative numbers is simpler than adding or subtracting. Multiply and divide as usual, then determine the sign of the product or quotient. If both of your numbers have the same sign, the product or quotient will be positive. If the numbers have different signs, the product or quotient will be negative:

- positive × positive = positive

    $3 \times 4 = 12$

- negative × negative = positive

    $-3 \times (-4) = 12$

- positive × negative = negative

    $3 \times (-4) = -12$

- negative × positive = negative

    $-3 \times 4 = -12$

- positive ÷ positive = positive

    $10 \div 5 = 2$

- negative ÷ negative = positive

    $-10 \div (-5) = 2$

- positive ÷ negative = negative

    $10 \div (-5) = -2$

- negative ÷ positive = negative

    $-10 \div 5 = -2$

 Watch Video 1.24, Multiplying and Dividing Negative Numbers, at **videos.ivyglobal.com.**

Practice Questions: Negative Numbers

1. $-10 + 8 =$

2. $5 + (-15) =$

3. $-4 - 7 =$

4. $3 - (-9) =$

5. $-1 + (-6) =$

6. $144 + (-214) =$

7. $9 - (-9) =$

8. $-8 - (-2) =$

9. $14 + (-14) =$

10. $-100 + 8100 =$

11. $6 \times (-3) =$

12. $-5 \times (-7) =$

13. $-24 \div 4 =$

14. $8 \times (-5) =$

15. $18 \div (-2) =$

16. $-32 \div (-4) =$

17. $-12 \times 2 =$

18. $-45 \div (-3) =$

19. $-120 \div 20 =$

20. $-25 \times (-4) =$

Section 9
Exponents and Roots

An **exponent** indicates that a number is being multiplied by itself. The exponent is the small, raised number to the right of the **base** (which is the number that is being multiplied by itself):

$$3^4 \leftarrow \text{Exponent}$$

$$\nearrow$$

Base

For this example, we would read "three to the power of four." **Squaring** a number means raising it to the power of two, and **cubing** a number means raising it to the power of three.

How to Solve Exponents

The exponent tells you how many times the base is being multiplied by itself. For example, 3^4 means that three is being multiplied by itself four times: $3^4 = 3 \times 3 \times 3 \times 3 = 81$.

You can apply the exponent to a negative number, a fraction, and even a variable and it will work the same way. For example, $\left(\frac{1}{4}\right)^2$ means to multiply $\frac{1}{4}$ by itself twice: $\left(\frac{1}{4}\right)^2 = \frac{1}{4} \times \frac{1}{4} = \frac{1}{16}$.

 Watch Video 1.25, Exponents, at **videos.ivyglobal.com.**

Roots

A **root** is the opposite of an exponent. A root is indicated by a **radical** placed over a **radicand**. This tells us that the radicand is the product of some other number multiplied by itself:

Radical $\longrightarrow \sqrt{16}$

$\nwarrow$

Radicand

For instance, the **square root** of a number is the opposite of squaring a number. To find a square root of a number underneath a radical, ask yourself, "What number can be multiplied by itself to produce the number in the question?" For example:

$$\sqrt{16} = 4 \text{ because } 4^2 = 4 \times 4 = 16$$

Similarly, the **cube root** of a number is the opposite of cubing a number. A cube root (or fourth root, fifth root, etc.) is indicated by a small raised number to the left of the radical:

$$\sqrt[3]{27} = 3 \text{ because } 3^3 = 3 \times 3 \times 3 = 27$$

You can take the square root (or cube root, or any root) of a fraction by taking the root of the numerator and the denominator separately:

$$\sqrt{\frac{16}{25}} = \frac{\sqrt{16}}{\sqrt{25}} = \frac{4}{5}$$

 Watch Video 1.26, Roots, at **videos.ivyglobal.com.**

Rules for Exponents: Upper Level Only

If you are multiplying two exponents with the same base, simply add their exponents:

$$4^2 \times 4^7 = 4^{2+7} = 4^9$$

Similarly, if you are dividing two exponents with the same base, subtract their exponents:

$$\frac{5^6}{5^2} = 5^{6-2} = 5^4$$

If you are raising an exponent to another power, multiply the two exponents:

$$(2^3)^2 = 2^{3 \times 2} = 2^6$$

Remember that these rules apply only to exponents with the same base! If you have two different bases, you cannot use these rules to simplify your exponents. Additionally, there is no way to simplify your exponents if you are adding or subtracting two numbers with exponents. These rules only apply to multiplication, division, or raising an exponent to another power.

Watch Video 1.27, Rules for Exponents, at **videos.ivyglobal.com.**

Rules for Roots: Upper Level Only

Unlike exponents, you can simplify roots by adding or subtracting. If both of your radicands (the numbers under the root) are the same, then you can combine them as you would a variable, by counting the number of roots and writing this number as a coefficient before your radical:

$$\sqrt{16} + \sqrt{16} = 2\sqrt{16}$$

If your roots already have coefficients, add or subtract these coefficients to come up with your sum or difference:

$$5\sqrt{4} - 2\sqrt{4} = 3\sqrt{4}$$

Remember that you can only add or subtract roots *with the same radicand.*

However, you can multiply or divide roots with different radicands. Multiply or divide the two radicands and write the quotient or product as your new radicand:

$$\sqrt{2} \times \sqrt{5} = \sqrt{2 \times 5} = \sqrt{10}$$

If your roots have coefficients, multiply or divide these as well:

$$4\sqrt{12} \div 2\sqrt{3} = (4 \div 2)\sqrt{12 \div 3} = 2\sqrt{4}$$

Watch Video 1.28, Rules for Roots, at **videos.ivyglobal.com.**

Practice Questions: Exponents and Roots

1. $7^2 =$ 49

2. $2^4 =$ 16

3. $5^3 =$ 75

4. $1^5 =$ 1

5. $\left(\dfrac{2}{3}\right)^3 =$ $\dfrac{8}{27}$

6. $\left(\dfrac{1}{2}\right)^4 =$ $\dfrac{1}{16}$

7. $(-10)^3 =$ 1000 $-10 \times -10 \times -10$

                                     $\underline{100} \times$

8. $(-9)^2 =$ 81

9. $\sqrt{100} =$ 10

10. $\sqrt{36} =$ 6

11. $\sqrt[3]{8} =$

12. $\sqrt[3]{64} =$

13. $\sqrt{\dfrac{4}{9}} =$

14. $\sqrt{\dfrac{1}{49}} =$

Questions 15-24 are Upper Level Only.

15. $2^2 \times 2^5 =$ 2^{10} $2 \times 2 \times 2 \times 2 \times 2 \times 2 \times 2 \times 2 \times 2 \times 2$ = (1,024)

16. $5^7 \div 5^5 =$ $5^2 = 25$

17. $\left(\dfrac{1}{3}\right)^2 \times \left(\dfrac{1}{3}\right)^3 =$ $\dfrac{1}{3}^5$

18. $(4^2)^2 =$ 4.4

19. $(2^3)^4 =$ $(8)^4$ $8 \times 8 \times 8 \times 8 =$ (4,096)

20. $\sqrt{5} + 4\sqrt{5} =$

21. $4\sqrt{2} - 3\sqrt{2} =$

22. $\sqrt{18} \div \sqrt{2} =$

23. $2\sqrt{3} \times 2\sqrt{12} =$

24. $\left(\sqrt[3]{9}\right)^3 =$

$\overset{3}{64}$
8
$5.1, 2$

$\overset{'}{512}$
8
(4096)

Exponents and Roots   123

Section 10
Order of Operations

If you have to solve an expression involving negative numbers, exponents, and parentheses, don't simply read from left to right! The **order of operations** tells you what to solve first:

1. Solve any expressions inside parentheses
2. Solve any exponents or roots
3. Multiply and divide from left to right
4. Add and subtract from left to right

These five steps (Parentheses, Exponents, Multiplication, Division, Addition, and Subtraction) can be remembered by the mnemonic PEMDAS or the phrase "Please Excuse My Dear Aunt Sally." For instance, let's solve this complicated expression:

Example

$$3 + 7 \times (6-4)^2 - 8 \div 2$$

1. Solve the parentheses:
$$3 + 7 \times (6-4)^2 - 8 \div 2 = 3 + 7 \times (2)^2 - 8 \div 2$$

2. Solve the exponents:
$$3 + 7 \times (2)^2 - 8 \div 2 = 3 + 7 \times 4 - 8 \div 2$$

3. Multiply and divide from left to right:
$$3 + 7 \times 4 - 8 \div 2 = 3 + 28 - 4$$

4. Add and subtract from left to right:
$$3 + 28 - 4 = 27$$

 Watch Video 1.29, Order of Operations, at **videos.ivyglobal.com.**

Practice Questions: Order of Operations

1. $4 \times (8 - 3) + 13 =$ $4(5) + 13 = 20 + 13 = \boxed{33}$

2. $5^2 - 3 \times 4 =$ $25 - 3 \times 4 = 25 - 12 = 13$

3. $8^2 - 3 \times (-4) =$ $64 - 3(-4)$ $64 + 12 = \boxed{76}$

4. $3 + 8^2 - (6 - 4) \times 12 =$ $3 + 64 - (2) \times 12$
   $3 + 64 - (24) = 67 - 24 = \boxed{43}$

5. $10^2 - (4 - 3) \times 100 =$ $100 - (1) \times 100$
   $100 - 100 = \boxed{0}$

6. $32 + 2^5 \div 16 =$ $32 + 16 \div 16 = 32 + 1 = 33$
   $2 \times 2^4 \times 2^5 2^{1} = \boxed{33}$

7. $4^2 - (-16 - 2) \times 10 =$ $16 - (-18) \times 10$
   $16 - (-180)$
   $16 + 180 = \boxed{196}$

8. $8 - 3 \times 4 + (5 - 17) =$ $8 - 3 \times 4 + (-12)$
   $8 - 12 + (-12)$
   $\boxed{8}$

9. $-3 + (1 - 7)^2 \div 3^2 =$
   $-3 + (-6)^2 \div 9$
   $-3 + (36) \div 9$ $-3 - 4 = \boxed{-7}$

10. $6 \times \sqrt{9} - (7^2 - 40) =$
    $6 \times 3 - (49 - 40) = 18 - (9) = \boxed{9}$

11. $2 + 2^4 \div 8 + (4 - 2) - (2 - 3) =$
    $2 + 16 \div 8 + (2) - (-1)$
    $2 + 2 + (2) + 1$ $2 + 2 + 2 + 1 = \boxed{7}$

12. $-3 \times 2^2 + 10 - (-2 - 6) =$

    $-3 \times 4 + 10 - (-8)$

    $-12 + 10 + 8$

    $-12 + 18$

    $\boxed{6}$

13. $5 \times \dfrac{1}{3^2} - \dfrac{1}{3} =$ $\dfrac{5}{1} \times \dfrac{1}{9} - \dfrac{1}{3}$ $\dfrac{5}{9} - \dfrac{1}{3} = \dfrac{4}{6} = \boxed{\dfrac{2}{3}}$

14. $\sqrt{(3+5)^2} - (6 \times 7 - 34) =$ $8 - (42 - 34)$
$8 - 8 = \boxed{0}$

15. $\sqrt{(9+1)^2 \div 4} =$
$100 - 4 = 25$ $= \boxed{5}$

16. $3 \times (-2)^2 + 15 \div 3 - (2 + 14) =$
$3 \times 4 + 5 - (16)$
$12 + 5 - 16$ $\boxed{1}$
$12 + -11 =$

17. $\sqrt{(-9)^2} - 2 \times 8 - 10 =$
$9 - 2 \times 18 - 10$ $-5 - 10$ $\boxed{-15}$
$9 - 16 - 10$

18. $\dfrac{1}{4} + 5 \times \dfrac{1}{2^2} - \dfrac{1}{2} \div 2 =$

$\dfrac{1}{4} + \dfrac{5}{4} - \dfrac{7}{4}$

$\boxed{\dfrac{7}{4}}$

Section 11
Arithmetic Review

1. $103 - 1\frac{2}{5} =$

    (A) $100\frac{3}{5}$

    (B) $101\frac{2}{5}$

    (C) $101\frac{3}{5}$

    (D) $102\frac{3}{5}$

    (E) $103\frac{2}{5}$

2. $468.3 \div 31.2$ is closest to

    (A) 1.5
    (B) 15
    (C) 150
    (D) 1500
    (E) 15000

3. $\frac{1}{2} \times 5.64 =$

    (A) 2.82
    (B) 3.32
    (C) 5.14
    (D) 6.14
    (E) 11.28

4. What is the least prime number greater than 30?

   (A) 31
   (B) 32
   (C) 35
   (D) 37
   (E) 39

5. $\dfrac{1}{100} + \dfrac{2}{200} + \dfrac{3}{300} =$

   (A) $\dfrac{6}{6,000,000}$

   (B) $\dfrac{6}{600}$

   (C) $\dfrac{1}{100}$

   (D) $\dfrac{3}{100}$

   (E) $\dfrac{6}{100}$

6. Out of the 40 games a soccer team played in one season, it lost 15 games, tied 5 games, and won the remaining games. What was the ratio of the team's wins to losses?

   (A) 2:1
   (B) 3:4
   (C) 4:3
   (D) 5:3
   (E) 40:15

7. Derek bought 1.4 pounds of bananas at $0.50 per pound, 2.5 pounds of oranges at $1.20 per pound, and 2 pounds of apples at $1.31 per pound. How much did he spend in total?

   (A) $2.59
   (B) $6.32
   (C) $6.81
   (D) $9.39
   (E) $17.55

8. Forty percent of 19.95 is closest to

   (A) 4
   (B) 5
   (C) 8
   (D) 10
   (E) 80

9. The highest peak of Mount Everest is about 29,030 feet above sea level, and the lowest point in the Dead Sea is about 1,310 feet below sea level. What is the difference in elevation between the lowest point of the Dead Sea and the highest peak of Mount Everest?

(A) 1,310 feet

(B) 27,720 feet

(C) 29,160 feet

(D) 30,340 feet

(E) 31,650 feet

10. What is the smallest number that can be added to 367 to produce a result divisible by 3?

(A) 1

(B) 2

(C) 3

(D) 4

(E) 5

11. Which of the following numbers is NOT prime?

(A) 2

(B) 3

(C) 5

(D) 7

(E) 9

12. If Jenny sleeps for 8 hours every day, she will spend the equivalent of how many days asleep over the course of one week?

(A) $\dfrac{1}{3}$

(B) $\dfrac{3}{8}$

(C) $\dfrac{4}{3}$

(D) $2\dfrac{1}{3}$

(E) $2\dfrac{1}{8}$

13. At 8:00am, the temperature was –10 degrees. If the temperature dropped 13 degrees over the next 12 hours, what was the temperature at 8:00pm?

(A) –23°

(B) –13°

(C) –3°

(D) 3°

(E) 23°

14. If N is a positive number, all of the following statements must be true EXCEPT

(A) $N - N = 0$

(B) $N \times \dfrac{1}{N} = 1$

(C) $N^1 = N$

(D) $N + N$ is a positive number

(E) N^2 is an even number

15. What is the greatest integer less than $\dfrac{83}{6}$?

(A) 11

(B) 12

(C) 13

(D) 14

(E) 15

16. $\sqrt{\dfrac{64}{4}}$

(A) $\dfrac{1}{16}$

(B) $\dfrac{1}{4}$

(C) 2

(D) 4

(E) 16

17. A museum exhibit charges $15.25 for an adult ticket and $9.50 for a child ticket. If 500 adults and 120 children visit the exhibit, the museum's ticket sales will total

    (A) $5,890
    (B) $6,580
    (C) $7,625
    (D) $8,765
    (E) $9,455

18. Which of the following is a multiple of 2, 3, and 5?

    (A) 123,450
    (B) 123,455
    (C) 123,460
    (D) 123,465
    (E) 123,470

19. Kathy works 3.5 hours a day on Mondays, Wednesdays, and Fridays, and 4.5 hours a day on Tuesdays and Thursdays. She is paid $10.20 per hour. If Kathy does not work on Saturdays or Sundays, how much does she earn in one week?

    (A) $15.75
    (B) $35.70
    (C) $81.60
    (D) $163.20
    (E) $198.90

20. Which of the following expressions is greatest?

    (A) $\dfrac{2}{5} + 2$

    (B) $\dfrac{9}{4} - \dfrac{1}{8}$

    (C) $\dfrac{21}{16} \div \dfrac{3}{4}$

    (D) $\dfrac{2}{5} \times \dfrac{5}{2}$

    (E) $\dfrac{10}{3} - 1$

21. $2^4 + 2^2 \div 2 - 2 =$

    (A) 1
    (B) 2
    (C) 8
    (D) 16
    (E) 32

22. A submarine was situated 260 feet below sea level. The submarine then ascended 120 feet. What was its new altitude?

   (A) 380 feet below sea level

   (B) 140 feet below sea level

   (C) 20 feet below sea level

   (D) 140 feet above sea level

   (E) 380 feet above sea level

23. A calculator has a price of $40, not including tax. After a 13% sales tax is applied, what will be the total cost of the calculator?

   (A) $5.20

   (B) $34.80

   (C) $41.30

   (D) $45.20

   (E) $53.00

24. The square root of 85 falls between what two integers?

   (A) 2 and 3

   (B) 4 and 5

   (C) 6 and 7

   (D) 8 and 9

   (E) 9 and 10

25. Which of the following is NOT less than 0.6?

   (A) $\dfrac{2}{9}$

   (B) $\dfrac{3}{13}$

   (C) $\dfrac{2}{3}$

   (D) $\dfrac{3}{6}$

   (E) $\dfrac{3}{7}$

26. Ms. Anderson's math class has 30 students. 60% of these students are boys, and 50% of these boys ride the bus to school. How many boys in Ms. Anderson's math class ride the bus to school?

   (A) 5

   (B) 6

   (C) 7

   (D) 8

   (E) 9

27. If Q is an even number, which of the following expressions must be odd?

(A) $2Q$

(B) Q^2

(C) $Q - Q$

(D) $Q - 3$

(E) $Q + 2$

28. During a chemistry experiment, a solution contained in a beaker was initially measured at 25 degrees Celsius. The beaker was then placed on a hot plate, and the temperature rose 7 degrees. Next, the beaker was submerged in an ice bath, and the temperature dropped 41 degrees. The final temperature of the solution was

(A) –23 degrees

(B) –16 degrees

(C) –9 degrees

(D) 32 degrees

(E) 73 degrees

29. $\dfrac{1}{2} \times \dfrac{2}{3} \times \dfrac{3}{4} \times \dfrac{4}{5} \times \dfrac{5}{6} \times \dfrac{6}{7} \times \dfrac{7}{8} \times \dfrac{8}{9} =$

(A) $\dfrac{1}{45}$

(B) $\dfrac{1}{9}$

(C) $\dfrac{40320}{362881}$

(D) $\dfrac{9}{11}$

(E) 1

30. On his last chemistry test, Mark answered 85% of the questions correctly and did not skip any questions. If there were 120 questions on the test, how many did he answer incorrectly?

(A) 15

(B) 18

(C) 35

(D) 42

(E) 102

31. If K has a factor of 15, K must also have what other factor(s)?

  (A) 5 only

  (B) 3 and 5

  (C) 0, 3 and 5

  (D) 1, 3, and 5

  (E) 0, 1, 3, and 5

32. $(8 - 17) \times 6 - \dfrac{1}{2} \times 4 =$

  (A) −218

  (B) −198

  (C) −56

  (D) 6

  (E) 54

33. Three consecutive multiples of 6 have a sum of 126. What is the greatest of these numbers?

  (A) 24

  (B) 36

  (C) 42

  (D) 48

  (E) 60

34. In a student art club with 48 members, the ratio of boys to girls is 3:5. One third of the girls in the art club are also members of another club. How many girls only participate in the art club?

  (A) 5

  (B) 10

  (C) 20

  (D) 30

  (E) 40

35. When N is divided by 16, the result is 7 with a remainder of 3. What is the remainder when N is divided by 5?

  (A) 0

  (B) 1

  (C) 2

  (D) 3

  (E) 4

36. 3 is 10% of

(A) 0.3

(B) 3

(C) 10

(D) 30

(E) 300

37. $2^6 =$

(A) 12^1

(B) 6^2

(C) 8^2

(D) 16^2

(E) 4^4

38. Susie's Superstore has 3 times as many wooden desks as plastic desks in its inventory. If the store only sells these two types of desks, which could be the total number of desks in stock?

(A) 10

(B) 25

(C) 38

(D) 44

(E) 71

39. A fast-food chain currently sells 8-ounce hamburgers. If the chain increases the weight of its hamburgers by 25%, the new hamburgers will weigh:

(A) 2 ounces

(B) 4 ounces

(C) 8.25 ounces

(D) 10 ounces

(E) 12 ounces

40. 100 students attended a school carnival. If 60% of the students were less than 10 years old and 75% of the students were over 6 years old, how many children were between 6 and 10 years old?

(A) 15

(B) 35

(C) 45

(D) 60

(E) 75

41. Between 1980 and 1990, the population of deer in a national park increased by 40%. Between 1990 and 2000, the deer population increased by 20%. The deer population in 2000 was how many times greater than the deer population in 1980?

    (A) 0.6
    (B) 1.6
    (C) 1.68
    (D) 60
    (E) 168

42. A pair of jeans is on sale for 60% off the original price. If the discounted price is $27.50, the original price was

    (A) $11.15
    (B) $16.50
    (C) $45.83
    (D) $68.75
    (E) $74.58

43. Anthony drove 53 kilometers. If 1 mile corresponds to about 1.6 kilometers, approximately how many miles did Anthony drive?

    (A) 16
    (B) 21
    (C) 33
    (D) 57
    (E) 85

44. $(\sqrt{5})^4 =$

    (A) 1
    (B) 2.2
    (C) 2.5
    (D) 5
    (E) 25

45. If 55% of N is 11, what is N% of 46?

    (A) 2.8
    (B) 5.1
    (C) 6.1
    (D) 9.2
    (E) 25.3

46. On a property valued at $310,000, the property tax is $24,800. A second property is valued at $340,000 with the same property tax rate. Including tax, the second property is how much more expensive than the first?

    (A) $27,270

    (B) $30,000

    (C) $32,400

    (D) $33,480

    (E) $57,270

47. $\sqrt{1200} =$

    (A) $60 \times \sqrt{2}$

    (B) $20 \times \sqrt{3}$

    (C) $4 \times \sqrt{30}$

    (D) $3 \times \sqrt{40}$

    (E) $1 \times \sqrt{12}$

48. The value of a coin collection increased 8% in the first year and 15% in the second year. By what percent did the collection's value increase over the entire two-year period?

    (A) 1.2%

    (B) 7%

    (C) 16.2%

    (D) 23%

    (E) 24.2%

49. $\left(\frac{1}{3}\right)^5 \div \left(\frac{1}{3}\right)^3 =$

    (A) $\frac{1}{15}$

    (B) $\frac{1}{9}$

    (C) $\frac{1}{3}$

    (D) $\frac{2}{5}$

    (E) $\frac{15}{9}$

50. Which of the following expressions is NOT equal to 7?

(A) $7^5 - 7^4$

(B) $7^2 \div 7$

(C) $\left(\sqrt[3]{7}\right)^3$

(D) $7^4 \times \dfrac{1}{7^3}$

(E) $\sqrt{7} \times \sqrt{7}$

Algebra

Section 1
Basic Algebra

Algebra is a branch of mathematics that uses letters to stand for numbers. These letters, called **variables**, represent numbers that are unknown. Any letter—*x, y, a, b, N, Q,* etc.—can be used to stand for unknown numbers. You can add, subtract, multiply or divide these variables just as you would any other number—the only difference is that you are working with letters!

Algebra is very useful for solving complex word problems. Putting a word problem into an algebraic expression or equation makes relationships much clearer and easier to solve in a systematic manner.

Basic Algebra Strategies

In some algebra questions, you could be given the value of a letter in the question, and will need to plug in this value to find the answer. For example, look at the following question:

Example

If $a = 3$, what is $a + 4$?

This question is telling you that the letter "a" stands for the number 3. To solve the question, plug in 3 where you see "a":

$$a + 4$$
$$3 + 4 = 7$$

Replacing the letter "a" with the number "3," we solve a normal addition problem and find the answer: 7. Here's another example:

Example

If $b = 5$ and $c = 6$, what is $c - b$?

This question is telling you that the letter "*b*" stands for the number 5, and the letter "*c*" stands for the number 6. To solve the question, plug in 6 where you see "*c*" and 5 where you see "*b*":

$$c - b$$
$$6 - 5 = 1$$

We can now solve a normal subtraction problem and find the answer: 1.

Finding a Missing Number

Some algebra problems may ask you to "work backward" and find the missing number in an equation. For example, look at the question below:

Example

$6 + \boxed{} = 20$

To find the missing number that goes in the box, ask yourself, "What plus 6 is equal to 20?" The answer is 14:

$$6 + \textbf{14} = 20$$

Instead of a box, the missing number in an equation might be represented by a letter. In this case, all you need to do is work backward to find what number this letter is standing for. For example, look at the question below:

Example

If $4 \times N = 8$, what is the value of N?

To find the number that N is standing for, ask yourself, "What can I multiply by 4 to get a result of 8?" The answer is 2:

$$4 \times \textbf{2} = 8$$

Therefore, we know that the value of N must be 2.

Formulas and Word Problems

Algebra is very useful for solving complex word problems. For example:

Example

John is building a rectangular patio in his backyard. If one of the sides of the patio must be 9 feet long, what length should John make the other side of the patio so that the patio has an area of exactly 36 square feet?

Because you know the area of a rectangle is equal to length multiplied by width, you can write an algebraic equation with the symbol x representing the missing side:

$$\text{Area} = \text{length} \times \text{width}$$
$$36 = 9 \times x$$

Based on this equation, you see that x was multiplied by 9 to get 36. Therefore, you need to divide 36 by 9 in order to find x, the length of your missing side:

$$x = 36 \div 9 = 4$$

Therefore, John should make the second side 4 feet long.

 Watch Video 2.1, Intro to Algebra, at **videos.ivyglobal.com.**

Practice Questions: Basic Algebra

1. If $N = 2$, what is the value of $N + 8$?

2. If $P = 6$, what is the value of $P + 7$?

3. If $m = 30$, what is the value of $m - 3$?

4. If $y = 10$, what is the value of $y - 10$?

For questions 5-12, solve each problem using the following information:

$$a = 4, b = 2, \text{ and } c = 8$$

5. $a + 4 =$

6. $b + 10 =$

7. $c - 3 =$

8. $a + b =$

9. $a \times 5 =$

10. $c \div 2 =$

11. $a \times b =$

12. $a - b + c =$

For questions 13-18, fill in the missing number:

13. $4 - \boxed{} = 2$

14. $\boxed{} \times 7 = 14$

15. $\boxed{} - 8 = 10$

16. $\boxed{} \div 4 = 3$

17. $8 + \boxed{} = 14$

18. $\boxed{} + 6 = 15$

19. If $4 + N = 7$, then $N =$

20. If $18 - p = 4$, then $p =$

21. If $Q \times 2 = 8$, then $Q =$

22. If $15 \div x = 3$, then $x =$

Section 2
Expressions

An algebraic **expression** is a mathematical "phrase" containing numbers, variables, and operations. In the example below, $9 \times x$ (which can also be written as $9x$) is an algebraic expression. There is no equals sign in an algebraic expression.

An algebraic expression is made up of **terms**, which are variables and/or numbers multiplied together. When a number is put right in front of a variable, it means the variable is being multiplied by that number—you don't have to write a multiplication sign. This number is called the **coefficient**.

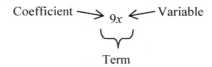

$$\text{Coefficient} \longrightarrow \underbrace{9x}_{\text{Term}} \longleftarrow \text{Variable}$$

An expression with one term only, like the one above, is called a **monomial**. The expression $4x + 6$ has two terms and is called a **binomial**. Any expression with more than one term is called a **polynomial**.

 Watch Video 2.2, Expression Terminology, at **videos.ivyglobal.com.**

Plugging In

You may be given the value of one or more variables and be asked to solve an algebraic expression based on these values. Plug these values into your expression and follow the order of operations.

For instance, take a look at the following problem:

Example

If $x = 2$ and $y = 3$, what is the value of $x^2 - 3y + 11$?

Plug in 2 for x and 3 for y, and use the order of operations to solve:

$$2^2 - 3 \times 3 + 11$$
$$= 4 - 3 \times 3 + 11$$
$$= 4 - 9 + 11$$
$$= 6$$

Simplifying Expressions with Addition and Subtraction

You can simplify an algebraic expression by adding or subtracting **like terms**. Like terms have variables that are raised to the same power. For example, $4x$ and $6x$ are like terms. The terms y^2 and $3y^2$ are also like terms. However, y and y^2 are not like terms because only one has been squared. Similarly, x^2 and y^2 are not like terms because they are two different variables.

To add or subtract like terms, add or subtract their coefficients. For example:

Example

What is the sum of $4N$ and $6N$?

To solve this question, add 4 and 6: $4N + 6N = 10N$

Remember that when a variable does not have a coefficient, it is the same thing as having a coefficient of one. The term N^2 is the same as $1N^2$, but we don't normally bother writing a coefficient of one. For example:

Example

Subtract N^2 from $3N^2$.

You would solve this by subtracting 1 from 3: $3N^2 - N^2 = 2N^2$

You can think of adding like terms as similar to adding groups of objects. For example:

> **Example**
>
> Emil had a bag of 3 apples and 4 oranges. He then bought another 5 apples and 3 oranges. How many apples and oranges does Emil have now?

To calculate your total, you add the numbers of apples together and the numbers of oranges together: 8 apples and 7 oranges. However, you can't add 3 apples to 3 oranges because these are two different types of fruit! Just as you can only add or subtract similar objects, you can only add or subtract like terms in algebra.

What if you are adding or subtracting expressions with more than one term? You would add or subtract the like terms, and leave any remaining terms as they are. For example:

> **Example**
>
> Add $P^2 + 6$ and $2P^2 + P - 4$.
>
> $$P^2 + 6 + 2P^2 + P - 4 = 3P^2 + P + 2$$

We have two pairs of like terms: P^2 and $2P^2$, and 6 and -4. Add these like terms together, and keep the term P the way it is.

 Watch Video 2.3, Simplifying Expressions with Multiplication and Division, at **videos.ivyglobal.com.**

Simplifying Expressions with Multiplication and Division: Upper Level Only

To multiply expressions, you need to use the **distributive property** of mathematics. According to the distributive property, multiplying a number by a sum of two other numbers in parentheses is the same as multiplying by each number separately and then adding:

$$a(b + c) = ab + ac$$

> **Example**
>
> Multiply the expression $3x + 2$ by the number 6.

To solve, use the distributive property: $6(3x + 2) = 6 \times 3x + 6 \times 2 = 18x + 12$

The distributive property also works for division. Dividing a sum of two numbers by another number is the same as dividing each number separately and then adding:

$$\frac{b + c}{a} = \frac{b}{a} + \frac{c}{a}$$

Example

Divide the expression $4y - 8$ by the number 2.

To solve, divide each term by 2: $\dfrac{4y - 8}{2} = \dfrac{4y}{2} - \dfrac{8}{2} = 2y - 4$

To multiply two monomials, you can use your knowledge of exponent rules to multiply terms with the same base.

Example

What is the product of x^2 and x^3?

To solve this problem, you would add the two exponents: $x^2 \times x^3 = x^{2+3} = x^5$

Similarly, to divide two terms in an equation that have the same base, you can subtract their exponents.

Example

Find the quotient: $4y^5 \div 2y^2$

In the example above, you would first divide the coefficients of each term, and then divide the variables themselves: $4y^5 \div 2y^2 = (4 \div 2)y^{5-2} = 2y^3$

If your terms do not have the same base, you can't add or subtract their exponents. Write the product or quotient of the individual terms:

Example

What is the product of x^2 and y^2?

Your terms do not have the same base, so write out the product with the individual terms:

$$x^2 \times y^2 = x^2 y^2$$

To multiply two polynomials, use the **FOIL** method: multiply the **F**irst terms, the **O**uter terms, the **I**nner terms, and the **L**ast terms. Then, combine like terms.

Example

Multiply $x + 2$ by $3x + 4$.

To simplify this expression, we'll first multiply together the first terms in the parentheses (x and $3x$), then the outer terms (x and 4), then the inner terms (2 and $3x$), and finally the last terms (2 and 4). Then, we'll add them together and combine last terms:

$$(x + 2)(3x + 4)$$

$$= (x \times 3x) + (x \times 4) + (2 \times 3x) + (2 \times 4)$$

$$= 3x^2 + 4x + 6x + 8$$

$$= 3x^2 + 10x + 8$$

 Watch Video 2.4, Simplifying Expressions with Multiplication and Division, at **videos.ivyglobal.com.**

Factoring Expressions: Upper Level Only

Factoring is the opposite of distribution. To factor a polynomial, find the greatest common factor that all of your terms have in common. Then, work backwards to take this factor out of your expression: write your factor multiplied by a polynomial in parentheses, and make sure that all of the terms inside of the parentheses multiplied by the factor generate the polynomial that you started out with.

Example

Factor $5x^2 - 10x + 30$.

In the expression above, all of your terms have a common factor of 5. Pull this factor out of your expression and determine what would be left over in parentheses:

$$5x^2 - 10x + 30 = 5(x^2 - 2x + 6)$$

To test whether you have factored correctly, use the distributive property to work backwards. Multiply your factor by the terms inside the parentheses and make sure that you get the same polynomial you started out with.

 Watch Video 2.5, Factoring Expressions, at **videos.ivyglobal.com.**

Practice Questions: Expressions

1. If $x = 5$, what is the value of $3x - 4$?

2. If $N = -2$, what is the value of $N^2 + 4N$?

3. If $a = 6$ and $b = 1$, what is the value of $7a - 20b$?

4. If $P = 3$ and $Q = 4$, what is the value of $2P^2 + 3Q - 4P$?

For questions 5-10, simplify the expressions by adding or subtracting like terms.

5. $2N + 3N =$

6. $x + 8x =$

7. $4a^2 - 2a^2 =$

8. $4h - 3h + 7 =$

9. $N + M + 2N =$

10. $3x^2 - y^2 - 2x^2 + 4y^2 =$

Questions 11-22 are Upper Level Only.

For questions 11-20, use the distributive property to multiply or divide the expressions.

11. $3(x^2 + 12) =$

12. $2(a^2 - 2a + 3b^2) =$

13. $x^2(2x + 8) =$

14. $5y(3y^2 - 2y + 10) =$

15. $(3g + 9) \div 3 =$

16. $(16x^2 + 24x) \div 4x =$

17. $(x + 5)(x + 2) =$

18. $(y - 4)(y + 10) =$

19. $(3a + 1)(a + 8) =$

20. $(4x + y)(x - 2y) =$

21. Factor the expression $16y + 4z$:

22. Factor the expression $12x^3 + 3x^2 - 9x$:

Section 3
Equations

An algebraic **equation** tells you that two expressions are equal to each other. In our backyard patio example in Section 1, we came up with a very simple equation telling us that $9x$ was equal to 36:

$$9x = 36$$

To solve an algebraic equation, we need to find a value for x that makes the equation true. For the equation above, we found that $x = 4$ because $9 \times 4 = 36$.

What if our equation is a little more complicated? Take a look at the equation below:

Example
$3x - 2 = 13$. Solve for x.

For this equation, we need to find a value for x that, when we multiply by 3 and subtract 2, equals 13. This equation takes a little more thought, but we soon find that $x = 5$ because $3 \times 5 - 2 = 13$.

Always check your answer! To do this, plug your answer back into the equation and check whether it makes the equation true.

Manipulating Equations: Upper Level Only

For many complicated algebraic equations, you will not be able to figure out the answer in your head; you will need to use a method to manipulate your equation and solve for the unknown variable. Your goal is always to **isolate** your variable—that is, to get your variable by itself on one side of the equation, and all of your numbers on the other side of the equation. To do this, work backwards to "undo" all of the operations that are being performed on your variable until you can get it by itself.

There is one important rule to remember when working with equations: *whatever you do to one side of the equation, you must also do to the other!* If you violate this rule, the two sides of your equation will no longer be equal. For example, let's consider this (obviously) true equation:

Example

$$4 = 4$$

If you add a number to one side of your equation but not to the other, the two sides are no longer equal:

$$4 = 4$$
$$4 + 2 \neq 4$$

You need to add the same number to *both* sides of your equation so they remain equal:

$$4 + 2 = 4 + 2$$

Let's see how this works with the equation we solved earlier:

Example

$$3x - 2 = 13$$

On the left side of the equation, x is being multiplied by 3, and 2 is being subtracted from the product. We need to "undo" each of these operations by adding numbers to and dividing numbers from both sides of our equation. When "undoing" operations, follow the order of operations backwards; that is, start with addition and subtraction, then multiplication and division, then exponents, and finally, parentheses. For this example, we first need to "undo" the subtraction by adding 2 to each side:

$$3x - 2 = 13$$
$$3x - 2 + 2 = 13 + 2$$
$$3x = 15$$

Then, we "undo" the multiplication by dividing each side by 3:

$$\frac{3x}{3} = \frac{15}{3}$$
$$x = 5$$

What if our equation has variables on both sides? First, we need to get all of the variables onto one side of the equation and combine like terms. Then, we can isolate our variable by adding, subtracting, multiplying, and dividing the same numbers on both sides of our equation.

For example, consider the equation:

Example

$$5a - 7 = 2a - 1$$

To solve for a, we first need to get all of our variables on one side of the equation by subtracting $2a$ from each side:

$$5a - 7 = 2a - 1$$
$$5a - 2a - 7 = 2a - 2a - 1$$
$$3a - 7 = -1$$

Then, we can "undo" the subtraction by adding 7 to each side:

$$3a - 7 + 7 = -1 + 7$$
$$3a = 6$$

And finally, we "undo" the multiplication by dividing each side by 3:

$$\frac{3a}{3} = \frac{6}{3}$$
$$a = 2$$

To test if we got the right answer, we can plug this number back into our equation to make sure that the equation holds true:

$$5a - 7 = 2a - 1$$
$$5 \times 2 - 7 = 2 \times 2 - 1$$
$$10 - 7 = 4 - 1$$
$$3 = 3$$

Because 3 does clearly equal 3, we know that our answer is correct.

 Watch Video 2.6, Intro to Equations, at **videos.ivyglobal.com.**

Practice Questions: Equations

Solve for x:

1. $x + 8 = 44$

2. $2x = 16$

3. $5 - x = 12$

4. $5x = -45$

5. $x \div 3 = 4$

6. $11x = 22$

7. $\frac{1}{2}x = 5$

8. $18 \div x = 6$

9. $4x - 2 = 18$

10. $-5x + 5 = 35$

Questions 11-20 are Upper Level Only.

Solve for x:

11. $7x - 3 = 6x + 8$

12. $4.5x = -63$

13. $x + 14 = 3x - 4$

14. $10x - 5 = x + 22$

15. $4x = -90 + x$

16. $8 - 3.2x = 6 - 3x$

17. $x \div 3 = x - 16$

18. $20 - 2x = \frac{1}{2}x$

19. $4(x - 5) = x + 1$

20. $3x + 42 = 2(4x + 11)$

Section 4
Inequalities

An **inequality** is a mathematical statement comparing two unequal quantities. We represent inequalities using the following symbols:

Inequality Symbols	
>	greater than
<	less than
≥	greater than or equal to
≤	less than or equal to

Example

11 is greater than 6.

Using a "greater than" symbol, we would write this as $11 > 6$.

An algebraic inequality states that a certain algebraic expression is greater than or less than another quantity. For instance:

Example

An unknown quantity, x, is less than 3.

We can express this statement with a "less than" symbol: $x < 3$.

There are many possible solutions for this inequality. For example, x might equal 1, 2, 0.5, –4, –6, 0, or any other number less than three.

If you have a more complex inequality, simply treat this inequality like an equation and find the simplest range of solutions for your variable. For example:

$$4N \geq 24$$

You would read this as "4 times N is greater than or equal to 24." You need to divide by 4 in order to find what N alone is greater than or equal to:

$$4N \geq 24$$
$$N \geq 6$$

If 4 times N is greater than or equal to 24, than N can be any value greater than or equal to 6.

 Watch Video 2.7, Intro to Inequalities, at **videos.ivyglobal.com.**

Rules for Inequalities: Upper Level Only

Like an equation, you can add or subtract the same number from both sides of an inequality and still preserve the inequality. For example:

$$x + 3 > 7$$

To solve this problem, we would subtract 3 from both sides of the inequality to solve for x:

$$x + 3 > 7$$
$$x + 3 - 3 > 7 - 3$$
$$x > 4$$

You have to be more careful when multiplying or dividing. Multiplying or dividing both sides of an inequality by a positive number preserves the inequality, but multiplying or dividing by a negative number *reverses* the inequality. For example, consider the following inequality:

$$5 > 3$$

We can multiply both sides of this inequality by a positive number, and the inequality is still true:

$$5 > 3$$
$$5 \times 4 > 3 \times 4$$
$$20 > 12$$

However, if we multiply both sides by a negative number, we get a false result:

$$5 > 3$$
$$5 \times (-4) > 3 \times (-4)$$
$$\cancel{-20 > -12}$$

Therefore, we need to *reverse* the inequality when multiplying or dividing by a negative number:

$$5 > 3$$
$$5 \times (-4) < 3 \times (-4)$$
$$-20 < -12$$

Let's try an example of a more complex algebraic inequality:

Example

$$-4x + 1 > 3$$

We approach this like an equation, and "undo" the addition by subtracting 1 from both sides:

$$-4x + 1 > 3$$
$$-4x + 1 - 1 > 3 - 1$$
$$-4x > 2$$

Then, we "undo" the multiplication by dividing both sides by –4, remembering to reverse the inequality because we are dividing by a negative number:

$$\frac{-4x}{-4} < \frac{2}{-4}$$
$$x < -\frac{1}{2}$$

Therefore, x can be any number less than $-\dfrac{1}{2}$. We can check our solution by picking a possible value for x and plugging it back into the original inequality. In this case, let's have x equal -1:

$$-4x + 1 > 3$$
$$-4 \times (-1) + 1 > 3$$
$$4 + 1 > 3$$
$$5 > 3$$

Because 5 is greater than 3, we know we have solved our inequality correctly.

 Watch Video 2.8, Rules for Inequalities, at **videos.ivyglobal.com.**

Practice Questions: Inequalities

1. If $x < 6$, can -1 be a possible value for x?

2. If $P \geq 4$, can 3 be a possible value for P?

3. If $N < 15$, can -10 be a possible value for N?

4. If $q \geq 10$, can 10 be a possible value for q?

5. If $2y \geq 20$, give one possible value for y:

6. If $d - 5 < 9$, give one possible value for d:

7. If $3 < a < 13$, give one possible value for a:

8. If $4x \leq 16$, give one possible value for x:

9. If $N + 2 \geq 9$, give one possible value for N:

10. If $3z > 27$, give one possible value for z:

Questions 11-20 are Upper Level Only.

Solve for x:

11. $7x \geq 21$

12. $x - 4 > 8$

13. $x + 16 \leq 15$

14. $-3x < 45$

15. $4x - 10 > -2$

16. $8 - 5x \leq -27$

17. $9x - 20 > 5x$

18. $3x + 7 \leq x + 1$

19. $16 < 4x < 24$

20. $23 \leq 7x + 2 \leq 37$

Section 5
Strange Symbols

The SSAT loves using strange symbols—stars, bubbles, smiley faces, etc.—to represent relationships among numbers and variables. These symbols always have a formula or rule that shows clearly what this relationship is. To solve a strange symbol question, simply look for the rule, and figure out what numbers you need to plug in.

For example, consider the following question:

Example

For any numbers N and M, $N \blacklozenge M = 2N + 3M$. What is the value of $4 \blacklozenge 1$?

In this question, the SSAT has used the symbol $\blacklozenge$ to represent a set of operations to perform on two numbers. The rule tells us that "one number $\blacklozenge$ another number means two times the first number plus three times the second number." Therefore, we only need to plug in 4 for the first number and 1 for the second number to answer the question:

$$4 \blacklozenge 1 = 2 \times 4 + 3 \times 1 = 11$$

Strange Symbols and Algebra

Strange symbol questions may also involve more complicated algebra. For example, consider the following question:

Example

For any number x, $⇧x = 2x - 4$. If $⇧h = 4$, what is the value of h?

This complicated-looking question is just an algebra problem in disguise. The rule tells you that to "$⇧$" a number means to multiply the number by 2 and subtract 4. Therefore, to find $⇧h$, all we need to do is plug h into the rule:

$$\Uparrow h = 2h - 4$$

We know that this expression must also equal 4, because the prompt tells us that $\Uparrow h = 4$.

Therefore, we can write a simple algebraic equation:

$$2h - 4 = 4$$

Working backwards, we can see that

$$2h = 8$$

And therefore,

$$h = 4$$

Remember, to solve a strange symbol question, all you need to do is look for the rule and figure out what numbers or variables to plug in.

 Watch Video 2.9, Strange Symbols, at **videos.ivyglobal.com.**

Practice Questions: Strange Symbols

1. For any number x, $\square x = 5x + 7$. What is the value of $\square 6$?

2. For any number y, $\square y = 3y^2$. What is the value of $\square 2 + \square 3$?

3. For any number a, $\downarrow a = 2a^2 - 1$. What is the value of $\downarrow 4$?

4. For any non-zero number N, $\maltese N = \dfrac{10}{N}$. What is the value of $\maltese 5 \times \maltese 1$?

5. For any numbers g and h, $g \mathcal{H} h = 5g - h$. What is the value of $5 \mathcal{H} 13$?

6. For any numbers j and k, $j \square k = 2 + jk$. What is the value of $-7 \square 2$?

7. For any non-zero numbers m and n, $m \odot n = \dfrac{2m}{n}$. What is the value of $8 \odot 4$?

8. For any number z, $\spadesuit z = 4z - 6$. What is the value of $\spadesuit 3 \times \spadesuit 4$?

9. For any positive numbers P and Q, $P \blacktriangle Q = \sqrt{P + Q}$. What is the value of $9 \blacktriangle 16$?

10. For any positive number m, $\clubsuit m$ is equal to the number of prime numbers less than m. What is the value of $\clubsuit 20$?

Questions 11-17 are Upper Level Only.

11. If y is a negative number, let $\diamondsuit y = 4y + 7$. If y is zero or a positive number, let $\diamondsuit y = 3y^2$. What is the value of $\diamondsuit 3 + \diamondsuit(-5)$?

12. For any number z, $\circledcirc z = 5z + 14$. If $\circledcirc x = 4$, what is the value of x?

13. For any number y, $\blacktriangleright y = y^2 + 1$. What is the value of $\blacktriangleright\blacktriangleright 3$?

14. For any number N, $\ominus N = \dfrac{8}{6 - N}$. If $\ominus P = 2$, what is the value of P?

15. For any number Q, $\blacktriangle Q = 2^Q$. What is the value of $\blacktriangle\blacktriangle 1$?

16. If x is a positive number, let $\maltese x = \sqrt{x}$. If x is zero or a negative number, let $\maltese x = x^2$. What is the value of $\maltese\maltese(-45)$?

17. For any non-zero numbers a and b, $a\triangle b = \dfrac{2a}{b}$. If $3\triangle 4 = x\triangle 2$, what is the value of x?

Section 6
Word Problems and Algebra

Many word problems can be solved by re-writing your question as a simple algebraic equation. For example, in Section 1, we used algebra to find the length of one of the sides of a rectangular patio. The patio's area needed to be 36 square feet, and one of its sides needed to be 9 feet long. We used the formula for the area of a rectangle to find x, the length of the side we were missing:

$$\text{Area} = \text{length} \times \text{width}$$
$$36 = 9 \times x$$
$$x = 4$$

Here is another useful formula to remember for this exam:

$$\text{Distance} = \text{Rate} \times \text{Time}$$

Example

What is the distance travelled by a train moving at 80 miles per hour for 4 hours?

We would solve this problem by plugging in 80 (the train's rate) and 4 (the train's time) into the formula above:

$$\text{Distance} = 80 \times 4 = 320$$

The train has travelled 320 miles.

Not all word problems will be as simple as plugging numbers into a formula. You will need to know some quick ways of translating plain English into the language of mathematics. The following chart gives some examples:

Translating English into Mathematics		
Word/Phrase	Translation	Symbol
is, was, has, will be	equals	=
more, total, increased by, exceeds, gained, older, farther, greater, sum	addition	+
less, decreased, lost, younger, fewer, difference	subtraction	−
of, product, times, each	multiplication	×
for, per, out of, quotient	division	÷
at least	greater than or equal to	≥
at most	less than or equal to	≤
what, how much, a number	unknown variable	x, y, n, etc.

Example

Five less than three times a number is equal to seven. What is the number?

Let's write this as an algebraic equation using our translation chart above. If we let our unknown number be x, then "three times a number" means $3x$, and "five less" means we need to subtract 5. This whole expression equals 7:

$$3x - 5 = 7$$

$x = 4$ because $3 \times 4 - 5 = 12 - 5 = 7$. Therefore, we know our missing number must be 4.

As another example, consider the following word problem:

Example

Each person in a certain town owns an average of 2 vehicles. If there are 1280 personal vehicles registered in the town, what is the town's population?

Let's write this as an equation, with the variable p representing the number of people. We know that each person in the town owns, on average, 2 vehicles. Because "each" means "multiply," the number of vehicles in the town would be equal to 2 times the number of people. There are 1280 vehicles in the town, so we would write:

$$1280 = 2p$$

What times 2 is equal to 1280? In order to solve this, we need to divide 1280 by two:

$$p = 1280 \div 2 = 640$$

Based on this equation, the town's population must be 640.

 Watch Video 2.10, Algebraic Word Problems, at **videos.ivyglobal.com.**

1. The quotient of 45 and a number is equal to nine. What is the number?

2. The sum of twice a number and three is equal to nineteen. What is the number?

3. Adam has four more than twice as many marbles as John. If John has 5 marbles, how many marbles does Adam have?

4. Joe drove 6 hours at an average of 40 miles per hour. How far did he travel?

5. A photocopy store charges $0.10 a page for black-and-white copies and twice as much for color copies. If Lisa has to photocopy 33 pages in black-and-white and 10 pages in color, how much will the store charge in total?

6. On Tuesday, a store sold twice as many scarves as it did on Monday. On Wednesday, the store sold 10 more scarves than it did on Tuesday. If M represents the number of scarves sold on Monday, which of the following expressions represents the number of scarves sold on Wednesday?

    (A) $M + 10$
    (B) $M - 10$
    (C) $2M + 10$
    (D) $2M - 10$
    (E) $10M + 2$

7. Three friends are renting a car and splitting the cost evenly. Each person has to contribute $40.12 towards the total cost of the car. Then, a fourth friend decides to join the group. If there are now four friends splitting the cost evenly, what is the new amount that each person has to contribute?

8. If seven less than three times N is equal to 14, then what is the value of two times N?

9. Jason is flying from New York, which is on Eastern Standard Time (EST), to San Francisco, which is on Pacific Standard Time (PST). Pacific Standard Time is three hours behind Eastern Standard Time. If Jason's flight leaves at 1:30pm EST from New York and arrives at 2:45pm PST in San Francisco, how long is his flight?

10. During their last soccer game, Erin scored three less than twice as many goals as Jennifer did. If J represents the number of goals that Jennifer scored, which of the following expressions shows the total number of goals scored by Jennifer and Erin?

    (A) $3 - 2J$
    (B) $3 + 2 + J$
    (C) $2J - 3$
    (D) $3J - 3$
    (E) $3J + 3$

11. Mark is one year younger than Janet. Janet is twice Amanda's age. If Amanda is 9 years old, how old is Mark?

12. Sarah biked 5 miles at an average of 15 miles per hour. Then, she biked 5 miles at an average of 10 miles per hour. How long did her trip take?

13. To celebrate her birthday, Amy wants to bring cupcakes for her class. Cupcakes cost $6.00 for one dozen, $4.50 for half a dozen, and $1.00 individually. If there are 23 students in Amy's class, what is the minimum cost to bring exactly one cupcake for each student?

14. After reading for 2 hours, Mike has finished $\frac{1}{4}$ of his book. If he continues to read at the same rate, how much longer will it take him to finish his book?

15. Susanne earns $10 per hour for the first 40 hours of work each week, and $15 per hour for any additional work over 40 hours. If she earned $520 last week, how many hours did she work?

16. One third of what number is equal to 20 more than 50% of 80?

17. The population of a certain country doubles every 20 years. If the population in 2000 was 1.5 million, what will the population be in 2060?

18. Joe has two more pencils than Derek. If Joe buys 3 more pencils, he will have twice as many pencils as Derek. How many pencils does Derek have?

Section 7
Algebra Review

1. If $P = 4$, then $7P =$

    (A) $7 + 4$

    (B) $7 - 4$

    (C) 7×4

    (D) $7 \div 4$

    (E) 74

2. If $16 - n = 8$, then $n =$

    (A) 2

    (B) 4

    (C) 8

    (D) 16

    (E) 24

3. If the sum of a number and 3 is equal to 9, what is the number?

    (A) 3

    (B) 6

    (C) 9

    (D) 12

    (E) 27

4. At a school basketball game, each ticket cost \$5. If x represents the number of people who attended the game, what is the total amount of money that the school earned from ticket sales?

    (A) 5 dollars

    (B) $x + 5$ dollars

    (C) $x - 5$ dollars

    (D) $5x$ dollars

    (E) $x/5$ dollars

5. If $3K = 15$, then $K =$

   (A) 3
   (B) 5
   (C) 12
   (D) 18
   (E) 45

6. Rashmi has four more pencils than twice the number of pencils that John has. If John has 6 pencils, how many pencils does Rashmi have?

   (A) 6
   (B) 10
   (C) 12
   (D) 14
   (E) 16

   $2J + 4 = R$
   $12 + 4 = 16R$

7. If $6 \times \square + 5 = 17$, what is the value of $\square$?

   (A) 2
   (B) 3
   (C) 6
   (D) 12
   (E) 19

   $6x + 5 = 17$
   $6x = 12$

   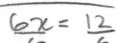

   $6x + 5 = 17$
   $\underline{ -5 \quad\;\; -5}$
   $6x = 12 \qquad x = 2$
   $6 \qquad 6$

8. Jane baked two muffins less than twice the number of muffins Adam baked. If m represents the number of muffins Adam baked, then the number of muffins Jane baked is

   (A) m
   (B) $2m$
   (C) $2m - 2$
   (D) $2m + 2$
   (E) $2m - 4$

   $2A - 2 = J$
   $2m - 2$
   $2m - 2$

9. If $x \leqslant 11$, then which of the following numbers is NOT a possible value of x?

   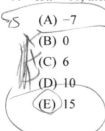

   (A) −7
   (B) 0
   (C) 6
   (D) 10
   (E) 15

10. Randy drove for three hours at an average speed of 30 miles per hour, and then for two hours at an average speed of 25 miles per hour. In total, how many miles did Randy drive?

(A) 50

(B) 55

(C) 90

(D) 135

(E) 140

11. If $7 - 5N = 12$, then $N =$

(A) −5

(B) −2

(C) −1

(D) 1

(E) 5

12. Rosa earns $12.50 per hour, and Emmanuel earns $15 per hour. If Emmanuel works 40 hours, how many hours does Rosa need to work in order to earn the same amount as Emmanuel?

(A) 2.5

(B) 42.5

(C) 43

(D) 48

(E) 500

13. If $\square + 2 = 6$, then $\square + 6 =$

(A) 3

(B) 4

(C) 10

(D) 12

(E) 16

14. "When 6 is subtracted from four times a number L, the result is 26." Which of the following equations represents this statement?

   (A) $4L = 26 - 6$

   (B) $4L - 6 = 26$

   (C) $L - 6 = 26 \times 4$

   (D) $4L + 6 = 26$

   (E) $4(L - 6) = 26$

$4L - 6 = 26$

$4L - 6 = 26$

15. If $\mathbf{5}y = 5y - 5$, what is the value of $\mathbf{5}4$?

   (A) 0

   (B) 4

   (C) 12

   (D) 15

   (E) 20

16. A convenience store charges $0.75 for each pack of gum and $1.25 for each chocolate bar. If Sandy buys two packs of gum and three chocolate bars, how much change does she receive from $10?

   (A) $0.00

   (B) $2.00

   (C) $4.75

   (D) $5.25

   (E) $8.00

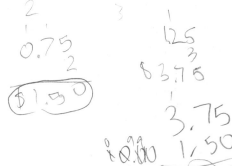

17. If $-2 \geq d$, then d could be

   (A) -2

   (B) -1

   (C) 0

   (D) 1

   (E) 2

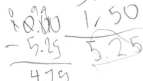

18. A carton is two-thirds full of juice. If one liter of juice is poured out, the carton will be one-half full. How many liters of juice will the carton hold when full?

   (A) 3

   (B) 6

   (C) 9

   (D) 12

   (E) 15

$\dfrac{2}{3}$ $\dfrac{1}{2}$

$\dfrac{4}{6}$ $\dfrac{3}{6}$

19. If $M \spadesuit N = MN + 4$, what is the value of $3 \spadesuit 12$?

    (A) 4
    (B) 15
    (C) 32
    (D) 36
    (E) 40

20. Kyle is six years younger than Milly, and Milly is four years older than twice Jerry's age. If Jerry is currently 12 years old, how old will Kyle be in three years?

    (A) 12
    (B) 22
    (C) 24
    (D) 25
    (E) 28

21. If $x = -2$, $y = 5$, and $z = -4$, what is the value of $x^2 + \frac{5}{y} - z$?

    (A) −9
    (B) −7
    (C) 1
    (D) 3
    (E) 9

22. If the sum of three consecutive integers is 27, what is the product of the three numbers?

    (A) 27
    (B) 90
    (C) 270
    (D) 720
    (E) 990

23. If $3K + 8 = 29$, then $K^2 =$

    (A) 7
    (B) 21
    (C) 25
    (D) 49
    (E) 81

24. Colleen ran for three miles at an average pace of 9 miles per hour, and then she ran an additional four miles at an average pace of 6 miles per hour. For how many total minutes did Colleen run?

(A) 60

(B) 70

(C) 80

(D) 90

(E) 100

25. If $-3 \leq \square < 5$, then which of the following numbers is NOT a possible value of $\square$?

(A) -3

(B) -1

(C) 0

(D) 3

(E) 5

26. If $x \copyright y = x^2 + y^2$, what is the value of $3 \copyright 4$?

(A) 12

(B) 16

(C) 25

(D) 48

(E) 144

27. Mr. Carson wants to buy notebooks for all of the 10 students in his English class. If notebooks cost $4.50 for a pack of six, $3.75 for a pack of three, and $2.00 for a single notebook, what is the least amount that Mr. Carson can spend to ensure that each student has at least one notebook?

(A) $4.50

(B) $9.00

(C) $10.25

(D) $12.00

(E) $20.00

28. If $c + d = 7$, then $3(c + d) =$

   (A) 10
   (B) 14
   (C) 21
   (D) 42
   (E) 56

29. If four more goldfish are added to a fish tank, there will be three times as many goldfish as there were last week, but only half as many as there were a year ago. If X goldfish are currently in the tank, which algebraic expression represents the number of goldfish in the tank a year ago?

   (A) $X + 4$
   (B) $2(X + 4)$
   (C) $(X + 4) \div 2$
   (D) $(X + 4) \div 3$
   (E) $(2X + 8) \div 3$

Questions 30-50 are Upper Level Only.

30. During their last basketball game, Carl scored three more than twice as many points as Craig. If B represents the number of points that Carl scored in the game, which of the following expressions represents the total number of points that both Carl and Craig scored in the game?

   (A) $2B$
   (B) $2B + 3$
   (C) $3B + 3$
   (D) $(B - 3) \div 2$
   (E) $(3B - 3) \div 2$

$$3B + 3$$

31. $7a + 14ab - 3a - 4a - 6a^2 - 2ab =$

   (A) $-6a^2 - 6ab + 7b$
   (B) $-6a^2 + 12ab + 14a$
   (C) $-6a^2 + 12ab$
   (D) $-6a^2 - 9ab$
   (E) $-6a^2$

$$7a + 14ab - 3a - 4a - 6a^2 - 2ab$$

$$7a - 3a - 4a + 12ab - 6a^2$$

$$14a + 12ab - 6a^2$$

$$-6a^2 + 12ab + 14a$$

32. Ahman has $4.75 in nickels, dimes, and quarters. If there are two times as many nickels as there are dimes, and there are three times as many quarters as there are dimes, how many dimes does Ahman have?

(A) 5

(B) 10

(C) 15

(D) 20

(E) 25

33. For what number N is the product of N and 2 equal to the sum of N and 2?

(A) -1

(B) 0

(C) 1

(D) 2

(E) 4

34. $-3x(-5xy + 7z) =$

(A) $35xy - 37xz$

(B) $-15xy^2 - 21x$

(C) $15x^2y - 21xz$

(D) $35x^2y - 21xz$

(E) $15xy - 21z$

35. Kevin runs for 45 minutes at an average speed of 8 miles per hour, rests for 5 minutes, and then returns home along his same route. If he only has 30 minutes after the end of his rest period to get home, what is the minimum average speed that he must run his return route?

(A) 4 miles per hour

(B) 8 miles per hour

(C) 10 miles per hour

(D) 12 miles per hour

(E) 14 miles per hour

36. $12g^2 - 24gh + 8g =$

(A) $2(6g^2 - 24gh + 8g)$

(B) $4(3g - 6h + 2g)$

(C) $4g(3 - 6h + 2g)$

(D) $4g(3g - 6h + 2)$

(E) $8g(4g - 3h + 1)$

37. $\dfrac{9a^7b^2c^4}{3a^3c^5} =$

    (A) $3a^4b^2c$

    (B) $\dfrac{a^4b^2}{c}$

    (C) $\dfrac{3a^4b^2}{c}$

    (D) $\dfrac{3a^4b}{c}$

    (E) $\dfrac{a^4b^2}{3c}$

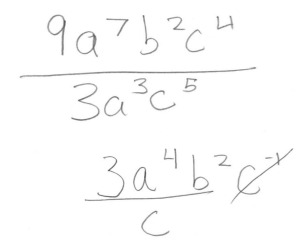

38. "The sum of twice a number P and 13 is less than the product of 4 and P." What is the lowest integer value for P that satisfies this expression?

    (A) 4

    (B) 7

    (C) 8

    (D) 9

    (E) 13

39. If $3N + 6 = N^2 + 8$, what could be a possible value of N?

    (A) 1

    (B) 3

    (C) 4

    (D) 5

    (E) 7

40. If $4z - 3 < 3z + 4$, then

    (A) $z > -7$

    (B) $z \le 7$

    (C) $z > 1$

    (D) $z < -1$

    (E) $z < 7$

41. $\dfrac{1}{2}(2K - 4)(3K - 2) =$

  (A) $6K^2 - 12K + 8$
  (B) $6K^2 - 14K + 8$
  (C) $6K^2 - 16K + 4$
  (D) $3K^2 - 8K + 4$
  (E) $3K^2 + 8K - 4$

42. Jason earns $8 per hour for the first eight hours of work each day, and $12 per hour for any additional daily work over eight hours. Charlotte earns $10 per hour, regardless of how many hours that she works each day. If on one day Jason and Charlotte work the same number of hours and earn $166 combined, how many hours did each of them work?

  (A) 7
  (B) 8
  (C) 9
  (D) 10
  (E) 18

43. If $6f + 12g + 2 = 8$, then $f + 2g =$

  (A) 1
  (B) 2
  (C) 3
  (D) 6
  (E) 10

44. If $66 \div a = 660b$, then $2ab =$

  (A) $\dfrac{1}{10}$
  (B) $\dfrac{1}{5}$
  (C) 5
  (D) 10
  (E) 20

45. In eight years, Nicole will be twice as old as her sister Jenny was two years ago, and half the age that Nicole's mother was when she got married. If Nicole's mother got married when she was 28, what is the difference in age between Nicole and her sister Jenny, in years?

(A) 3

(B) 6

(C) 7

(D) 9

(E) 14

46. If $4\left(\frac{1}{2}x - 1\right) + 2 = 7x - 1$, what is the value of x?

(A) $-\frac{1}{7}$

(B) $-\frac{1}{5}$

(C) $\frac{1}{6}$

(D) $\frac{2}{5}$

(E) 6

47. If $2c - 2 > 3(c + 4)$, then which of the following is not a possible value of c?

(A) -28

(B) -24

(C) -20

(D) -16

(E) -14

48. The number of mice in an apartment building is directly proportional to the number of apartment residents, and increases at a rate equal to six times the number of residents. If there are currently 66 mice in the apartment building, how many mice will be in the building if seven new residents move in?

(A) 66

(B) 73

(C) 102

(D) 108

(E) 114

49. For what value of K does $\dfrac{2}{K+2} = \dfrac{3}{K-1}$?

    (A) -8

    (B) -6

    (C) 2

    (D) 4

    (E) 6

50. If $x - 3 = 5y + 4$, then $x + 8 =$

    (A) $5y$

    (B) $5y + 1$

    (C) $5y + 7$

    (D) $5y + 15$

    (E) $y + 3$

Geometry

Section 1
Lines and Angles

A line is a straight, one-dimensional object: it has infinite length but no width. Between any two points, you can draw exactly one line that stretches in both directions forever. For instance, between the points A and B below, you can draw the line $\overleftrightarrow{AB}$. We name a line by drawing a horizontal bar with two arrows over two points on the line.

Line Segments and Midpoints

A **line segment** is a portion of a line with a finite length. The two ends of a line segment are called **endpoints**. For instance, in the figure below, the points M and N are the endpoints of the line segment $\overline{MN}$. We name a line segment with a plain horizontal bar over its two endpoints.

The point that divides a line segment into two equal pieces is called its **midpoint**. For instance, in the figure below, the point Q is the midpoint of the line segment $\overline{PR}$.

Because Q is the midpoint, it divides the segment into two equal pieces. Thus, we know $\overline{PQ} = \overline{QR}$.

You might be asked to find the length of a line segment based on the sum of its parts, or to find the length of one part of a line segment based on its total length.

For example, consider the following question:

In the figure below, B is the midpoint of $\overline{AC}$ and C is the midpoint of $\overline{AD}$. If $\overline{AD} = 12$, what is the length of $\overline{AB}$?

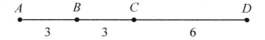

If C is the midpoint of $\overline{AD}$, this means that C divides $\overline{AD}$ into two equal segments: $AC = CD$. We're told that $AD = 12$, which means that $AC = 6$ and $CD = 6$.

We also know that B is the midpoint of $\overline{AC}$, which means that $AB = BC$. If $AC = 6$, we know that $BC = 3$ and $AB = 3$.

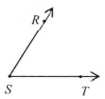 Watch Video 3.1, Lines and Line Segments, at **videos.ivyglobal.com.**

Angles

An **angle** is formed when two lines or line segments intersect. The point where the lines meet is called the **vertex** of the angle, and the two sides of the angle are called the **legs**. An angle can be named either with a single letter representing its vertex, or by three letters representing three points that define the angle: a point on one of its legs, the vertex, and a point on the other leg. In this case, the vertex is always in the middle. For example, the angle below can be called $\angle RST$ or simply $\angle S$.

Angles are measured in degrees from $0°$ to $360°$, which represents a full circle. Angles can be classified according to their degree measurements. Two angles that have equal measures are called **congruent**.

- An **acute** angle measures less than $90°$.
- A **right** angle measures exactly $90°$.
- An **obtuse** angle measures between $90°$ and $180°$.
- A **straight** angle measures exactly $180°$.

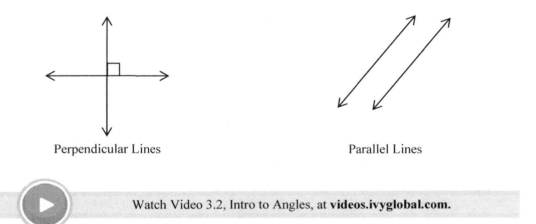

Acute   Right   Obtuse   Straight

Perpendicular and Parallel Lines

Two lines are **perpendicular** if they intersect to form a right angle. Right angles are often designated by a small square in the corner of the angle. If two lines are **parallel**, then they will never intersect.

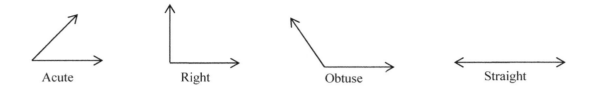

Perpendicular Lines   Parallel Lines

Watch Video 3.2, Intro to Angles, at **videos.ivyglobal.com.**

Complementary and Supplementary Angles

Here are some facts to know about angle sums:

- The sum of any number of angles that form a straight line is 180°.
- The sum of any number of angles around a point is 360°.
- Angles that add up to 90° are called **complementary angles**.
- Angles that add up to 180° are called **supplementary angles**.

Complementary Angles   Supplementary Angles

Bisecting Angles

A line that **bisects** an angle divides it into two equal parts. In the figure below, line $\overleftrightarrow{BD}$ bisects $\angle ABC$ and divides it into two congruent angles, $\angle ABD$ and $\angle DBC$:

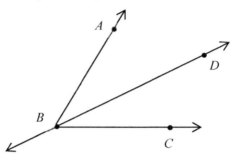

You may be asked to find the sum of several angles, or to find the measure of one angle based on the sum of several angles. For example, consider the following question:

Example

In the figure below, four angles intersect to form a straight line. If $\angle GFH$ and $\angle HFJ$ are complementary, and line $\overleftrightarrow{FK}$ bisects $\angle JFL$, what is the measure of $\angle KFL$?

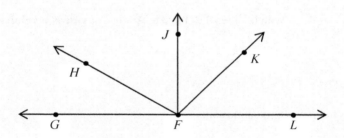

We know that any number of angles forming a straight line add up to 180°. Therefore, we can write:

$$\angle GFH + \angle HFJ + \angle JFK + \angle KFL = 180°$$

We are also told that $\angle GFH$ and $\angle HFJ$ are complementary, which means that they add up to 90°:

$$\angle GFH + \angle HFJ = 90°$$

If $\angle GFH$ and $\angle HFJ$ add up to 90°, this means that $\angle JFK$ and $\angle KFL$ also add up to 90°:

$$90° + \angle JFK + \angle KFL = 180°$$

$$\angle JFK + \angle KFL = 180° - 90° = 90°$$

Finally, we are told that line $\overleftrightarrow{FK}$ bisects $\angle JFL$, which means that $\angle JFK$ and $\angle KFL$ are congruent. If $\angle JFK$ and $\angle KFL$ are congruent and add up to 90°, then $\angle KFL$ must equal $90° \div 2 = 45°$.

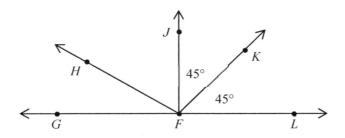

Watch Video 3.3, Angle Sums, at **videos.ivyglobal.com.**

Properties of Intersecting Lines: Upper Level Only

Two intersecting lines form two sets of **vertical angles**, which are congruent. In the figure below, $a = d$ and $b = c$.

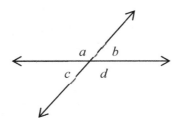

If a third line (**transversal**) intersects a pair of parallel lines, it forms eight angles, as in the following figure:

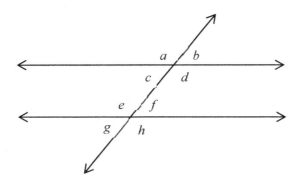

Know the following properties of transversals:

- The pairs of **corresponding** angles are congruent: $a = e$, $b = f$, $c = g$, and $d = h$.
- The pairs of **alternate interior** angles are congruent: $c = f$ and $d = e$.
- The pairs of **alternate exterior** angles are congruent: $a = h$ and $b = g$.
- The pairs of **same side interior** angles are supplementary: $c + e = 180°$ and $d + f = 180°$.

For example, consider the following question:

In the figure below, line m and line n are parallel, and line p bisects $\angle RST$. What is the value of x?

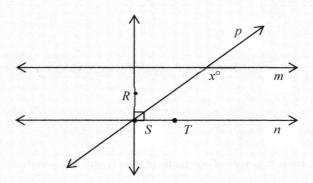

Based on the figure, we can see that $\angle RST$ is a right angle and therefore measures $90°$. If line p bisects this angle, it must divide it into two angles measuring $45°$ each. We can label these on the figure.

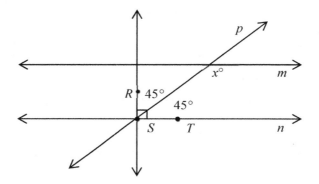

Because line p intersects two parallel lines, we know that pairs of same-side interior angles are supplementary. Thus, we know that $x°$ and $45°$ must add to equal $180°$. We can write an algebraic equation and solve for x:

$$x + 45 = 180$$

$$x + 45 - 45 = 180 - 45$$

$$x = 135$$

 Watch Video 3.4, Properties of Intersecting Lines, at **videos.ivyglobal.com.**

Practice Questions: Lines and Angles

1. In the figure below, $\overline{KM}$ = 5. If $\overline{LM}$ = 3, what is the length of $\overline{KL}$?

2. In the figure below, G is the midpoint of $\overline{FH}$. If $\overline{FG}$ = 4, what is the length of $\overline{FH}$?

3. In the figure below, R is the midpoint of $\overline{QS}$, and S is the midpoint of $\overline{QT}$. If $\overline{QR}$ = 2, what is the length of $\overline{RT}$?

4. In the figure below, angles CDE and EDF are complementary. If $\angle CDE$ measures 20°, what is the measure of $\angle EDF$?

    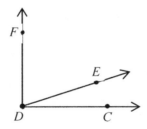

5. In the figure below, angle GHI is a right angle and b = 50°. if $a = c$, what is the value of c?

    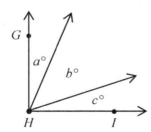

6. In the figure below, line $\overleftrightarrow{NO}$ bisects $\angle MNP$. If $\angle MNO$ measures 60°, what is the measure of $\angle MNP$?

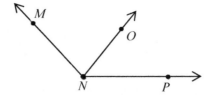

7. In the figure below, $\angle HJK$, $\angle KJL$, and $\angle LJM$ are supplementary. If $\angle LJM$ measures 70° and line $\overleftrightarrow{JK}$ bisects $\angle HJL$, what is the measure of $\angle KJL$?

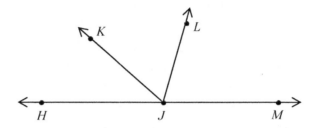

8. The three angles in the figure below form a straight line. If $y = 120°$, what is the value of $x + z$?

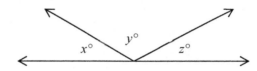

9. In the figure below, four lines intersect in point R to form four angles, and $\angle PRT$ is congruent to $\angle TRS$. If $\angle PRQ$ is a right angle, and $\angle QRT$ measures 150°, what is the value of $\angle TRS$?

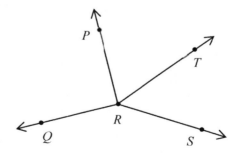

10. In the figure below, five lines intersect in a point to form five angles, If $a = 170°$ and $b = 60°$, what is the value of $c + d + e$?

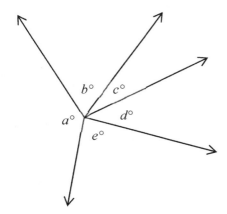

Questions 11-18 are Upper Level Only.

11. In the following diagram, two lines intersect to form four angles. If $x = 30°$, what is the value of y?

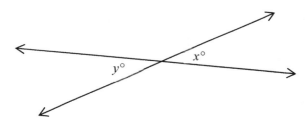

12. In the following diagram, lines m and n are parallel. If $a = 70°$, what is the value of b?

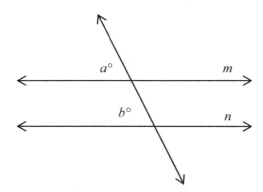

13. In the following diagram, lines *g* and *h* are parallel. If *z* = 120°, what is the value of *y*?

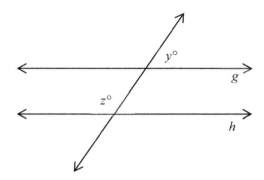

14. In the following diagram, lines *j* and *k* are parallel. If *c* = 50°, what is the value of *d*?

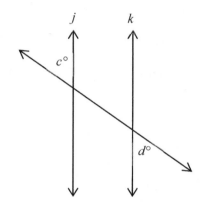

15. In the following diagram, lines *d* and *e* are parallel. What is the value of *x*?

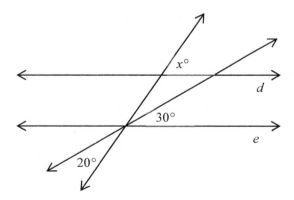

16. In the following diagram, lines p and q are parallel, and lines r and s are parallel. What is the value of $a + b + c + d$?

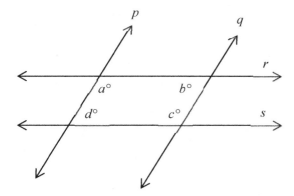

17. In the following diagram, lines l and m are parallel and are both perpendicular to lines n. What is the value of y?

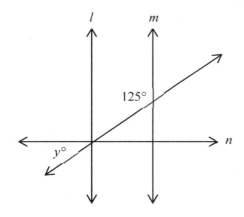

18. In the following diagram, lines u and v are parallel. What is the value of g?

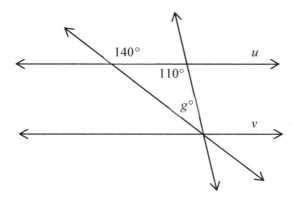

Section 2
Polygons

Properties of Polygons

A **polygon** is an enclosed two-dimensional shape with straight edges. "Poly" means "many" and "gon" comes from the Greek word for "angle," so a polygon is literally a "many-angled" shape. An **interior angle** of a polygon is an angle formed by the intersection of two sides. A **vertex** of a polygon is a point where two sides meet.

Polygons can be classified by the number of their sides:

Types of Polygons					
Name	Number of Sides	Example	Name	Number of Sides	Example
Triangle	3	△	Hexagon	6	⬡
Quadrilateral	4	▢	Heptagon	7	⬡
Pentagon	5	⬠	Octagon	8	⯃

In a polygon, equal sides are often marked with matching dash marks. For example, the diagram below shows a quadrilateral with two pairs of equal sides. The longer sides (with one dash mark) have equal lengths, and the shorter sides (with two dash marks) also have equal lengths.

A **regular polygon** has all equal sides and all equal angles. For example, a square is a regular quadrilateral because it has four equal sides and four equal angles.

Congruent and Similar Polygons

Two polygons are considered **congruent** if they have the same size and shape. The number of their sides will be the same, the lengths of their corresponding sides will be equal, and the measures of their corresponding interior angles will be equal. For example, the following trapezoids are congruent because they are identical in shape and in size. One just happens to be rotated.

Congruent Polygons

Two polygons are considered **similar** if they have the same shape, but not the same size. The number of their sides will be the same, the measures of their corresponding interior angles will be equal, and the lengths of their corresponding sides will be proportional—that is, they will maintain the same ratio. For example, the two triangles below are similar because their angles are the same and their sides maintain the same ratio of 3:4:5. One just happens to be twice as large.

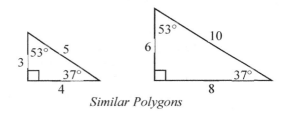

Similar Polygons

Perimeter

The **perimeter** of any polygon is the distance around its sides. To find the perimeter of a polygon, add together the lengths of its sides. For instance, the perimeter of the polygon below is equal to $3 + 6 + 6 + 1 + 3 + 5 = 24$.

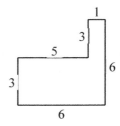

 Watch Video 3.5, Intro to Polygons, at **videos.ivyglobal.com.**

Math Review

Triangles
Part 1

Angles of a Triangle

The sum of the interior angles of a triangle is 180°. For example, in the following figure, we can calculate the missing interior angle:

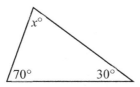

To find x, all we need to do is subtract 70 and 30 from 180: $x = 180 - 70 - 30 = 80$. The missing angle measures 80°.

Triangles can be classified according to the lengths of their sides and the measures of their angles:

- An **equilateral** triangle has three equal sides and three congruent angles. All three of these angles measure 60°.
- An **isosceles** triangle has two equal sides and two congruent angles across from these sides.
- A **scalene** triangle has three sides of different lengths and three angles of different measures.
- A **right** triangle has one angle measuring 90°.

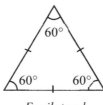

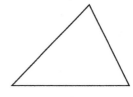

Equilateral	*Isosceles*	*Scalene*	*Right*

You can use your knowledge of the types of triangles to solve for missing angles. If you know your triangle is isosceles and you are given one of the angles, you can use this information to solve for the other two angles.

For example:

Example

In the triangle below, what is the value of *x*?

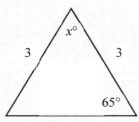

In the example above, we know we have an isosceles triangle because both sides are the same length. We also know the two angles opposite these sides must be the same length.

Because our triangle is isosceles, we know that the other corresponding angle also measures 65°:

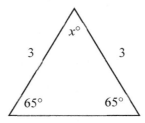

Because the sum of all angles in a triangle is 180°, we can solve for *x* by subtracting both angles from 180°:

$$x = 180 - 65 - 65 = 50$$

Our missing angle measures 50°.

Area of a Triangle

The **area** of a triangle can be found by multiplying one half the length of its base by its height, which is drawn perpendicular to its base:

$$\text{Area} = \frac{1}{2}\text{base} \times \text{height}$$

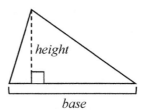

An obtuse triangle (a triangle with one obtuse angle) might have its height located *outside* of the triangle. For example:

Example

What is the area of the triangle below?

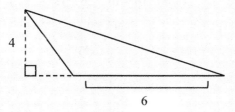

Even though it is located outside of the triangle, 4 is the height of the triangle because it is perpendicular to the base. We can find the area of the triangle by multiplying one half the length of the base times the height:

$$\text{Area} = \frac{1}{2} \times 6 \times 4 = 12$$

The area of the triangle is 12.

 Watch Video 3.6, Intro to Triangles, at **videos.ivyglobal.com.**

Solving Right Triangles: Upper Level Only

The **hypotenuse** of a right triangle is the side opposite the right angle. If the two legs of a right triangle have lengths a and b and the hypotenuse has a length c, then the **Pythagorean Theorem** states that

$$a^2 + b^2 = c^2$$

We can use this formula to solve for the missing side of a right triangle.

Example

What is the value of x?

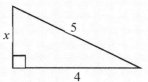

To find the length of the missing side, we plug the lengths of the two sides given into the Pythagorean Theorem, which states that the sum of the lengths of our two sides squared is equal to the length of the hypotenuse squared. Then, we solve for x:

$$x^2 + 4^2 = 5^2$$
$$x^2 + 16 = 25$$
$$x^2 + 16 - 16 = 25 - 16$$
$$x^2 = 9$$
$$x = \sqrt{9}$$
$$x = 3$$

 Watch Video 3.7, Solving Right Triangles, at **videos.ivyglobal.com.**

Quadrilaterals

Part 2

Angles of Quadrilaterals

The sum of the interior angles of any quadrilateral is 360°. For example:

What is the value of x?

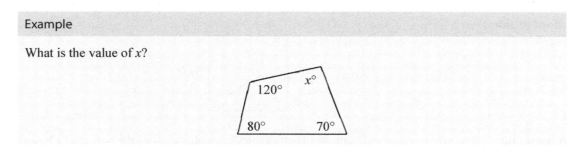

Because the sum of all angles in a quadrilateral is 360°, we can solve for x by subtracting the three given angles from 360°:

$$x = 360 - 120 - 80 - 70 = 90$$

Our missing angle measures 90°.

Types and Areas of Quadrilaterals

A **parallelogram** is a quadrilateral with two sets of parallel sides. The opposite sides and opposite angles of a parallelogram are equal. You can find the area of a parallelogram by multiplying the length of its base by its height (a line drawn perpendicular to the base):

Area = base × height

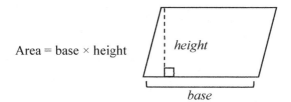

A **rectangle** is a parallelogram with four right angles. You can find the area of a rectangle by multiplying its length by its width:

Area = length × width

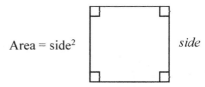

width

length

A **square** is a rectangle with four equal sides. A square is a regular quadrilateral—that is, all sides are the same length and all angles are the same measure (90°). You can find the area of a square by squaring one of its sides:

Area = side^2

side

A **trapezoid** is a quadrilateral with only one set of parallel sides, which are called the trapezoid's **bases**. You can find the area of a trapezoid by multiplying one half of the height by the sum of the lengths of the two bases:

$$\text{Area} = \frac{1}{2} \times \text{height} \times (\text{base 1} + \text{base 2})$$

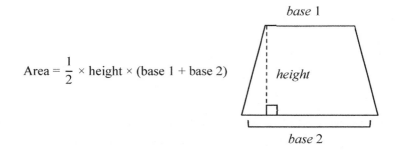

base 1

height

base 2

 Watch Video 3.8, Quadrilaterals, at **videos.ivyglobal.com**.

Practice Questions: Polygons

1. What is the perimeter of the triangle below?

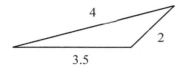

2. What is the perimeter of the polygon below?

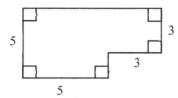

3. If an equilateral octagon has a total perimeter of 48, how long is each side?

4. What is the perimeter of the isosceles triangle below?

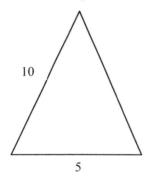

5. What is the area of the triangle below?

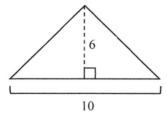

6. What is the area of the rectangle below?

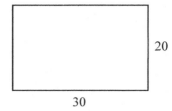

20

30

7. If the rectangle below has an area of 95, what is the value of *y*?

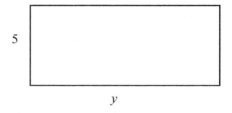

5

y

8. What is the area of a square with a side length of 9?

9. If the area of the triangle below is 12, what is the value of *x*?

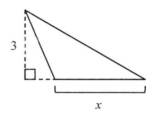

3

x

10. What is the area of the parallelogram below?

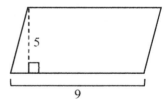

5

9

11. If the area of a square is 64 inches squared, what is the length of one of its sides?

12. What is the area of the shaded region below?

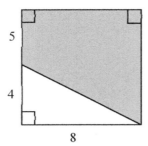

13. What is the area of the trapezoid below?

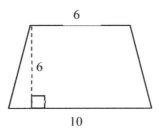

14. What is the area of the figure below?

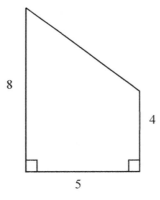

15. In the figure below, triangle *LMP* is an equilateral triangle, and *MNOP* is a square. If *NO* = 4 and the area of the entire figure is 22, what is the height *h* of triangle *LMP*?

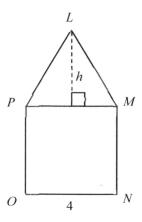

16. Triangle *ABC* is equilateral. What is the measure of angle *B*?

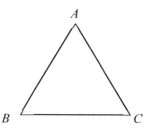

17. In trapezoid *NOPQ*, ∠*N* and ∠*O* are right angles, and ∠*P* measures 130°. What is the measure of ∠*Q*?

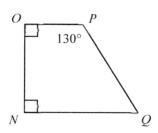

18. In the triangle below, $XY = YZ$, and $\angle Y$ measures 110°. What is the measure of $\angle Z$?

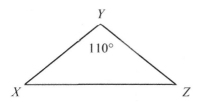

19. Triangle FGH is an isosceles right triangle. What is the measure of angle G?

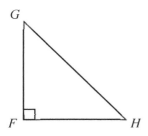

Questions 20-22 are Upper Level Only.

20. Triangle CDE is a right triangle. If $\overline{CD} = 3$ and $\overline{EC} = 4$, what is the length of $\overline{DE}$?

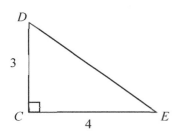

21. Triangle RST is a right triangle. If $\overline{RS} = 8$ and $\overline{ST} = 10$, what is the length of $\overline{TR}$?

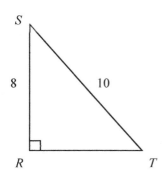

22. If the square below has an area of 50, what is the value of x?

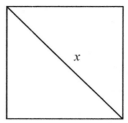

Section 3
Circles

A **circle** is a two-dimensional figure composed of points that are all the same distance from its center. The distance from the center of the circle to any point on the edge of the circle is called a **radius** (plural: radii). All radii of a circle are the same length.

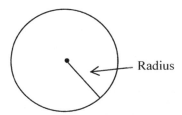

A **diameter** of a circle is a line that connects two points on the circle and passes through its center. The diameter of a circle is equal to twice the length of its radius. All diameters of a circle are the same length.

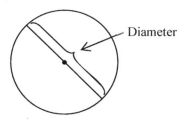

Circumference and Area of Circles: Upper Level Only

The **circumference** of a circle is the distance around the circle. It can be found by multiplying the diameter by π **(pi)**, a special number equal to approximately 3.14:

$$\text{circumference} = \text{diameter} \times \pi$$

Because π is a non-repeating, non-ending decimal number (3.1415927…), we frequently leave the symbol π as it is when calculating the circumference or area of a circle. This gives a more accurate answer than rounding a lengthy decimal number.

Calculate the circumference of the circle below.

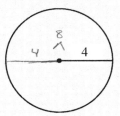

To do this, we find the diameter (twice the radius) and then multiply by π:

$$\text{circumference} = \text{diameter} \times \pi = 2 \times 4 \times \pi = 8\pi$$

If we wanted to find a decimal number for this circumference, we would multiply 8 by 3.14159… and get approximately 25.13. However, it is standard to leave 8π as the answer.

To find the **area** of a circle, multiply π by the radius squared:

$$\text{area} = \pi \times \text{radius}^2$$

Find the area of the circle below.

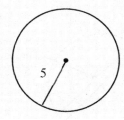

In order to solve this problem, square the radius and multiply by π:

$$\text{area} = \pi \times \text{radius}^2 = \pi \times 5^2 = 25\pi$$

It is standard to leave 25π as your answer, but you could also multiply by a close approximation of π to get about 78.54.

 Watch Video 3.9, Circles, at **videos.ivyglobal.com.**

Math Review

Practice Questions: Circles

1. What is the diameter of a circle with a radius of 3 inches?

    6   inches

2. What is the radius of a circle with a diameter of 20 centimeters?

    10   Centimeters

3. What is the radius of the circle below?

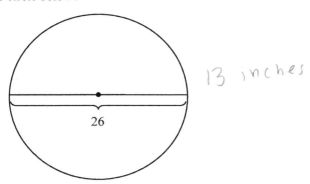

    13 inches

4. What is the diameter of the circle below?

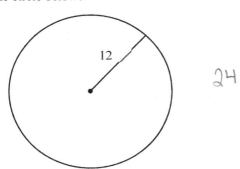

    24

5. If the two circles in the figure below each have a radius of 2, and both centers of those circles lie on the line $\overleftrightarrow{AB}$, what is the distance between point A and point B?

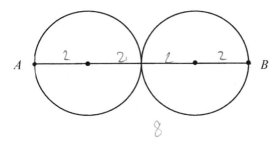

    8

6. Triangle *EFG* is formed by connecting the centers of circles *E*, *F*, and *G*. Each of these circles touches the other two circles at exactly one point. If all three circles have a radius of 5, what is the perimeter of triangle *EFG*?

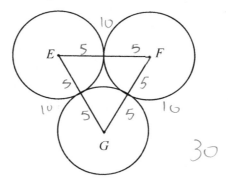

30

7. Square *RSTU* touches circle *V* at exactly one point on each side. If circle *V* has a radius of 3, what is the area of square *RSTU*?

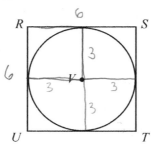

36 area

8. How many non-overlapping circles with a 2-inch radius can be drawn inside the rectangle below?

?

16 in.

8 in.

State your answer in terms of π instead of rounding.

9. What is the area of a circle with a radius of 4 meters?

$$A = \pi r^2 \qquad A = \pi\, 4^2 \qquad \boxed{A = 16\pi}$$

10. What is the circumference of a circle with a diameter of 10 inches?

$$C = \pi d \qquad C = \pi\, 10 \qquad \boxed{C = 10\pi}$$

11. What is the area of the circle below?

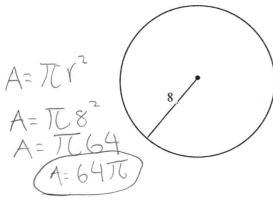

$$A = \pi r^2$$
$$A = \pi\, 8^2$$
$$A = \pi\, 64$$
$$\boxed{A = 64\pi}$$

12. If the area of a circle is 49π, what is its diameter?

$$A = \pi r^2 \qquad 49\pi \qquad 7 \times 7 \qquad \boxed{D = 14}$$

13. What is the circumference of the circle below?

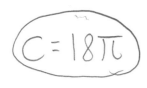

$$C = \pi d \qquad\qquad \boxed{C = 18\pi}$$

14. If the circumference of a circle is 36π, what is its diameter?

$$C = 36\pi \quad C = \pi d \qquad D = 36$$

15. If the area of a circle is 100π, what is its circumference?

$$A = \pi r^2 \qquad A = 100\pi$$
$$A = \pi\, 10 \times 10$$
$$C = \pi d$$
$$\boxed{C = 20\pi}$$

16. A goat is tethered to a fence with a 6-foot long rope. He can move within a semicircular region bounded by the fence, as shown below. What is the area of this region?

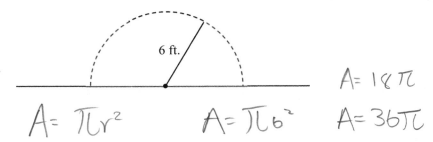

6 ft.

$A = \pi r^2$ $A = \pi 6^2$ $A = 18\pi$

$A = 36\pi$

17. In the figure below, a dart board is formed with three circles that share a center, each spaced 2 inches apart. If the area of the smallest circle is 9π inches squared, what is the circumference of the largest circle?

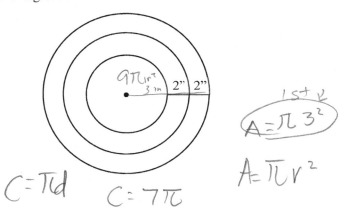

$9\pi in^2$
$3 in$ 2" 2"

$C = \pi d$ $C = 7\pi$

1st ↓
$A = \pi 3^2$

$A = \pi r^2$

18. In the figure below, square ABCD touches circle E at exactly one point on each side. If the perimeter of the square is 40, what is the area of the shaded region?

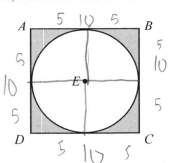

5   10   5
A   B
5   5
10   E•   10
5   5
D   C
5   10   5

>

Section 4
Solid Geometry

A **solid** is a three-dimensional object that has a length, width, and height. The **volume** of a solid is the region contained within the solid. The **surface area** of a solid is the area of its exterior surfaces.

Prisms
Part 1

A **prism** is any solid with two congruent polygons, called **bases**, joined by perpendicular rectangles. Each exterior surface of a prism is called a **face**, the lines where these faces intersect are called **edges**, and the points where these edges intersect are called **vertices** (singular: vertex).

Prisms are classified by the shape of their bases:

Types of Prisms		
Name	Shape of Base	Example
Triangular Prism	Triangle	
Rectangular Prism	Rectangle	
Pentagonal Prism	Pentagon	
Hexagonal Prism	Hexagon	

Surface Area of Prisms

The surface area of any prism can be found by adding together the areas of its faces.

For example, consider the following question:

Example

The figure below shows the dimensions for a cardboard box. If there are no overlapping sides, how many square inches of cardboard are needed to make this box?

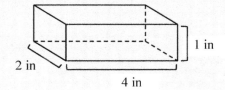

2 in

1 in

4 in

This question is asking us to find the surface area of a rectangular prism with a height of 1 inch, a width of 2 inches, and a length of 4 inches. To find how many square inches of cardboard make up the exterior of the box, we need to find the area of each rectangular face and then add these areas together. Remember that the area of a rectangle equals length times width:

$$\text{area} = \text{length} \times \text{width}$$

We'll calculate the area of each face by multiplying its length times its width. The areas of the front and back faces are each 4 in × 1 in = 4 in². The areas of the left and right faces are each 2 in × 1 in = 2 in². The areas of the top and bottom faces are each 4 in × 2 in = 8 in².

To find the total surface area of the box, we'll add together the areas of each of these faces:

$$\text{surface area} = \text{areas of front} + \text{back} + \text{left} + \text{right} + \text{top} + \text{bottom faces}$$

$$= 4 + 4 + 2 + 2 + 8 + 8 = 28 \text{ in}^2$$

The total surface area of the box is 28 in², which means that it will take 28 in² of cardboard to make.

Volume of Prisms

To find the volume of a rectangular prism, multiply its length by its width by its height:

$$\text{Volume} = \text{length} \times \text{width} \times \text{height}$$

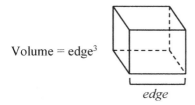

Example

What is the volume of a box that measures 5 feet by 3 feet by 10 feet?

To find the volume of this box, multiply 5 ft × 3 ft × 10 ft = 150 ft³.

A **cube** is a special type of rectangular prism with squares for all six faces. The length, width, and height of a cube are equal, so the volume can be found by cubing the length of one of its edges:

$$\text{Volume} = \text{edge}^3$$

edge

The volume of any other type of prism can be found by multiplying the area of one of its bases by its height, or the length of the edge perpendicular to its bases.

Example

Find the volume of the triangular prism below:

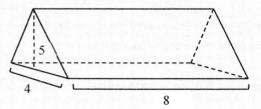

To find the volume, first find the area of its triangular base by multiplying one half of 4 by 5. Then multiply by its height (8):

$$\left(\frac{1}{2} \times 4 \times 5\right) \times 8 = 10 \times 8 = 80.$$

The volume of our triangular prism is 80.

 Watch Video 3.10, Intro to Solid Geometry, at **videos.ivyglobal.com.**

Cylinders: Upper Level Only
Part 2

A **cylinder** is like a prism, but its base is a circle instead of a polygon. A cylinder is formed by two circular bases connected by a perpendicular curved surface.

Surface Area of Cylinders

To find the surface area of a cylinder, imagine that the cylinder was sliced along its height and "unfolded" on a flat surface. You would then have two circular bases and one rectangle that normally wraps around the bases. To find the surface area of the cylinder, you need to add up the areas of the bases ($2\pi r^2$) and the area of this rectangle.

This rectangle has a length that is equal to the circumference of one of the bases, and a width that is equal to the height of the cylinder. Thus, to find the area of this rectangle, you would multiply the cylinder's circumference by its height. You would then add this number to the area of the two bases to find the total surface area of the cylinder:

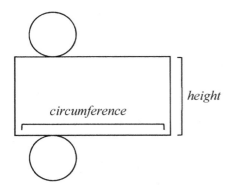

Surface area = (area of bases) + (circumference × height)

Example

Find the surface area of the cylinder below.

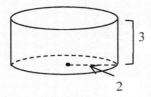

To solve this problem, first find the area of the bases. Each base has an area equal to π times 2 squared:

$$\text{Area of each base} = \pi \times 2^2 = 4\pi$$

$$\text{Area of both bases} = 4\pi + 4\pi = 8\pi$$

Then, find the circumference by multiplying 2 times π times the radius:

$$\text{Circumference} = 2 \times \pi \times 2 = 4\pi$$

Finally, find the area of the curved rectangular surface by multiplying the circumference by the height (3), and add this value to the area of the bases to find the total surface area of the cylinder:

$$\text{Surface area} = (\text{area of bases}) + (\text{circumference} \times \text{height})$$

$$= (8\pi) + (4\pi \times 3)$$

$$= 8\pi + 12\pi = 20\pi$$

The total surface area of the cylinder is 20π.

Volume of Cylinders

The volume of a cylinder is equal to the area of its base multiplied by its height:

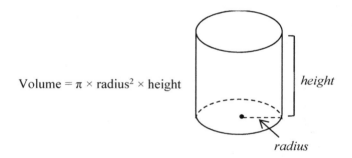

$$\text{Volume} = \pi \times \text{radius}^2 \times \text{height}$$

Example

What is the volume of the cylinder below?

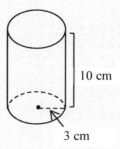

10 cm

3 cm

First, find the area of the cylinder's base (π times 3 squared) and multiply by its height (10):

$$\text{Volume} = \pi \times \text{radius}^2 \times \text{height}$$
$$= \pi \times 3^3 \times 10$$
$$= \pi \times 9 \times 10 = 90\pi$$

The volume of the cylinder is 90π cubic centimetres.

Watch Video 3.11, Cylinders, at **videos.ivyglobal.com.**

Other Solids: Spheres, Pyramids, and Cones
Part 3

You will not need to know how to calculate the volume or surface area of the following solids, but you may need to know some of their properties.

A **sphere** is like a three-dimensional circle: it is a collection of points in space all the same distance away from the center. As in a circle, this distance is called the sphere's radius, and all radii of a sphere are equal.

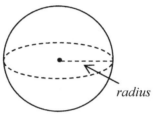

A **pyramid** has a polygon for a base and triangular faces that join in a point, called the **vertex** of the pyramid. The distance between a pyramid's base and its vertex is called its height. Like prisms, pyramids are named after the shape of their bases. For instance, a triangular pyramid has a triangle for its base, a rectangular pyramid has a rectangle for its base, and so on.

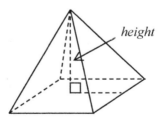

A **cone** is like a pyramid, but it has a circle for a base and a curved surface that tapers to a point, which is also called its vertex. The height of a cone is the distance between its base and its vertex.

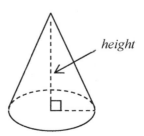

Nets

Part 4

A **net** is a two-dimensional figure formed by "unfolding" a solid along its edges. Nets can be useful to help you calculate the surface area of a solid. For instance, the figure below is a net of a rectangular pyramid:

Example

Find the total surface area of the pyramid below.

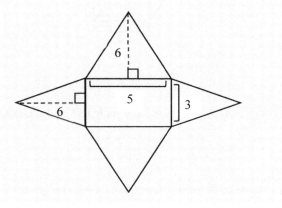

If this net were cut out and folded into a solid, it would form a pyramid with a rectangular base measuring 5 × 3.

To calculate the surface area of this pyramid, we need to calculate the area of the net above. The area of the rectangular base is 3 × 5 = 15. The area of each of the larger triangles is half their base (5) multiplied by their height (6): $\frac{1}{2}$ × 5 × 6 = 15. The smaller triangles each have a base of 3 and a height of 6, so their area is $\frac{1}{2}$ × 3 × 6 = 9.

To find the total surface area of the pyramid, we need to add together the area of each of these polygons:

$$Total\ area = 15 + (2 \times 15) + (2 \times 9) = 63$$

The total area of this net, and therefore the surface area of the pyramid, is 63 square units.

Practice Questions: Solid Geometry

1. What is the volume of the box below?

    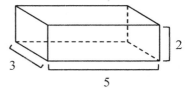

2. What is the volume of the cube below?

    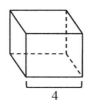

3. If a box has a volume of 48 cubic feet, and its length and width each measure 4 feet, what is its height?

4. If a cube has a volume of 27 cubic meters, what is the length of one of its edges?

5. Jake is painting the outside of a cube that measures 6 inches on each edge. How many square inches of paint will he need?

6. How many edges does a pentagonal prism have?

7. What is the surface area of a rectangular prism with a height of 7, a width of 5, and a length of 4?

8. Amy is ordering wallpaper for her bedroom, which is 10 feet long by 12 feet wide by 9 feet high. If she wants to completely cover all four walls of her room with wallpaper, how many square feet of wallpaper will she need?

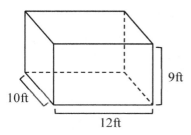

9. What is the volume of the triangular prism below?

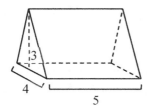

10. If the triangular prism below has a volume of 24, what is the value of x?

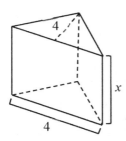

11. A tent manufacturer makes outdoor tents that are 6 meters wide, 4 meters tall, and 12 meters long, as shown below. The walls and the front and back of the tent are made out of canvas held up by a frame, and the bottom of the tent is open. How many square meters of canvas are needed to construct one tent?

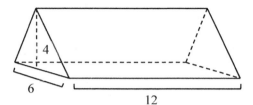

12. A cereal manufacturer ships its cereal boxes in plastic bins that measure 1 meter long, 1 meter wide, and 1.8 meters high. If each cereal box is 30 centimeters long, 5 centimeters wide, and 40 centimeters tall, how many boxes will fit into one plastic bin?

13. A manufacturer of tennis balls wants to package them in rectangular boxes that will fit 40 tennis balls each. If each tennis ball has a diameter of 3 inches, what is the smallest possible volume, in inches cubed, for each box?

14. All of the edges of the net below are 5 cm. If this net is cut out and folded along its edges to make a solid, what will its volume be?

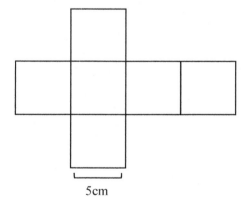

5cm

15. If the total surface area of a cube is 150 cm², what is its volume?

State your answer in terms of π instead of rounding.

16. What is the volume of the cylinder below?

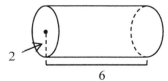

17. What is the surface area of a cylinder with a radius of 5 cm and a height of 8 cm?

18. For a school project, Jerry needs to construct an open tube out of paper with a length of 20 centimeters and a diameter of 5 centimeters. How many square centimeters of paper will he need to construct this tube?

19. A golf ball manufacturer packages golf balls in clear cylindrical containers, as shown below. If each golf ball has a diameter of 2 inches, what is the volume of the smallest possible cylindrical container that will fit 4 golf balls?

20. Company A and B both sell soda in aluminum cans. Company A's cans have a diameter of 3 inches and a height of 5 inches, and Company B's cans have diameter of 2 inches and a height of 4 inches. How many more square inches of aluminum per can are used by Company A than by Company B?

Section 5
Coordinate Geometry

Coordinate geometry is the study of points, lines, and shapes in the coordinate plane. A **plane** is a flat, 2-dimensional surface that has no defined width or length—it stretches forever in both directions.

The **coordinate plane** is formed by two perpendicular number lines called **axes** (singular: axis). The horizontal number line is called the **x-axis** because it is marked with the letter *x*. The vertical number line is called the **y-axis** because it is marked with the letter *y*. The point where the two axes intersect is called the **origin**, where both axes have the value of zero:

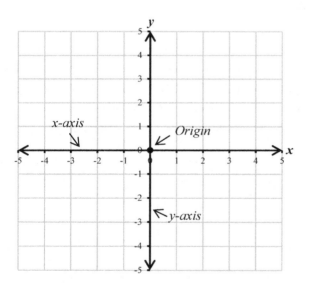

As the diagram shows, values on the *x*-axis are positive to the right of the origin and negative to the left of the origin. Values on the *y*-axis are positive above the origin and negative below the origin:

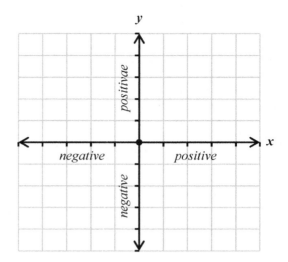

Points in the Coordinate Plane

As you saw in the previous diagram, the x- and y-axes intersect to form a grid. You can find the location of any point on this grid if you know two numbers: the point's horizontal distance away from the y-axis and vertical distance away from the x-axis. These two numbers are called its **coordinates**. The **x-coordinate** tells you the point's horizontal location along the x-axis, and the **y-coordinate** tells you the point's vertical location along the y-axis.

The coordinates for a point are normally written in parentheses, with the x-coordinate first and the y-coordinate second. This standard way of writing coordinates is called an **ordered pair**. If your point's coordinates were given by the ordered pair (3, 2), this means that 3 is your point's x-coordinate and 2 is your point's y-coordinate. Therefore, your point is a distance of 3 units to the right of the origin and 2 units above it. You would plot this point by finding the intersection of 3 on the x-axis and 2 on the y-axis:

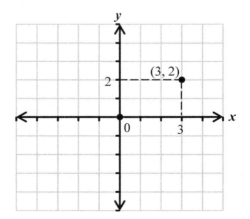

Remember that negative values along the *x*-axis are found to the left of the origin, and negative values along the *y*-axis are found below the origin. Therefore, if your point has the coordinates (−1, −4), you would plot this point 1 unit to the left of the origin and 4 units below the origin:

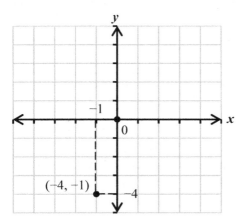

Quadrants

The axes of the coordinate plane divide it into four areas called **quadrants**. These are numbered counter-clockwise beginning with the top right quadrant:

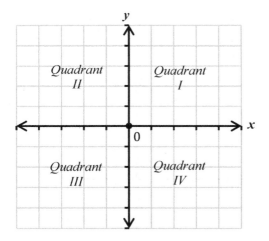

If you know what quadrant a point is in, you know whether its coordinates are positive or negative. For example, both the *x*- and *y*-coordinates of any point in Quadrant I are positive, and both the *x*-and *y*-coordinates of any point in Quadrant III are negative. Here is a chart that summarizes this information:

Quadrants in the Coordinate Plane		
	x-coordinates	*y*-coordinates
Quadrant I	+	+
Quadrant II	–	+
Quadrant III	–	–
Quadrant IV	+	–

With this information, you can find the coordinates of any point as long as you know its quadrant and its horizontal and vertical distance away from the origin.

Example

A point in Quadrant IV is 2 horizontal units and 5 vertical units away from the origin. Plot this point on a graph on a separate piece of paper.

If you were just told that the point is 2 horizontal units and 5 vertical units away from the origin, you wouldn't know whether these coordinates should be positive or negative. But since you were told that the point is in Quadrant IV, you know its *x*-coordinate will be positive and its *y*-coordinate will be negative, so its coordinates must be $(2, -5)$:

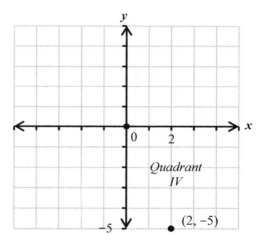

 Watch Video 3.12, Intro to Coordinate Geometry, at **videos.ivyglobal.com.**

Length and Area in the Coordinate Plane

You may be asked to find the length of a line segment drawn in the coordinate plane. To find the length of a horizontal line segment, calculate the difference between its two x-coordinates. To find the length of a vertical line segment, calculate the difference between its y-coordinates. For example:

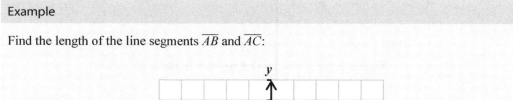

Find the length of the line segments $\overline{AB}$ and $\overline{AC}$:

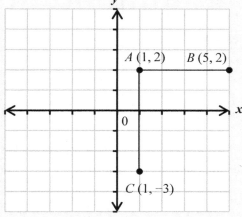

The x-coordinates of the horizontal line segment $\overline{AB}$ are 1 and 5, so the length of $\overline{AB}$ is $5 - 1 = 4$ units. The y-coordinates of the vertical line segment $\overline{AC}$ are 2 and -3, so the length of $\overline{AC}$ is $2 - (-3) = 5$ units.

It doesn't matter in which order you choose to subtract, but remember that the length of a segment is always positive. If you end up with a negative number, just reverse the sign. And if this sounds too complicated, remember that you're only dealing with number lines—you can always double-check your work by counting the spaces between two points!

You can use your knowledge of distances in the coordinate plane in order to calculate the areas of polygons. For example:

Find the area of triangle *JKL* below.

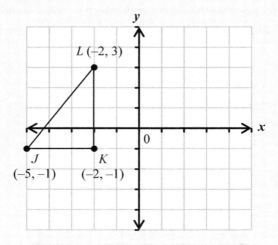

To find the area of triangle *JKL*, we need to find the length of its base and height. Its base is the horizontal line segment $\overline{JK}$, and we can find the length of $\overline{JK}$ by subtracting the *x*-coordinates of points *J* and *K*:

$$JK = -2 - (-5) = 3$$

The height of the triangle is the vertical line segment $\overline{KL}$, and we can find the length of $\overline{KL}$ by subtracting the *y*-coordinates of points *K* and *L*:

$$KL = 3 - (-1) = 4$$

Now that we know that the base of the triangle is 3 and the height is 4, we can use our formula for finding the area of a triangle:

$$\text{Area} = \frac{1}{2} \times 3 \times 4 = 6$$

The area of triangle *JKL* is 6 square units.

 Watch Video 3.13, Length and Area in the Coordinate Plane, at **videos.ivyglobal.com.**

Distance Using the Pythagorean Theorem: Upper Level Only

What if you were asked the following question about the previous figure?

Example

What is the length of the line segment JL in triangle JKL?

This is not a horizontal or vertical line segment, so you can't simply take the difference of the x- or y-coordinates.

However, JL is the hypotenuse of a right triangle, so you can use the Pythagorean Theorem:

$$a^2 + b^2 = c^2$$

In the part above, we determined that the two legs of the triangle, $\overline{JK}$ and $\overline{KL}$, had lengths of 3 and 4, respectively. We can square these lengths and add them together to get the square of the hypotenuse, then solve for the missing length:

$$JK^2 + KL^2 = JL^2$$
$$3^2 + 4^2 = JL^2$$
$$25 = JL^2$$
$$JL = \sqrt{25}$$
$$JL = 5$$

Therefore, the line segment $\overline{JL}$ is 5 units long. (For a review on solving right triangles with the Pythagorean Theorem, see Geometry, Section 2, in this math review).

This method can be used to find the length of any line segment in the coordinate plane. Even if the line segment is not the hypotenuse of a right triangle, you can draw an imaginary right triangle and use these imaginary sides to solve for the length of your segment. For example:

What is the length of the line segment $\overline{MN}$ in the diagram below?

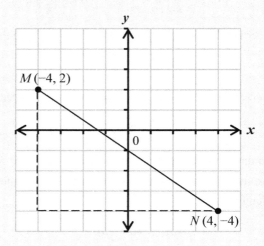

The dotted lines above show the legs of the imaginary right triangle that we have drawn with $\overline{MN}$ as its hypotenuse. To find the length of the horizontal leg, we can just subtract the x-coordinates of M and N: $4 - (-4) = 8$ units. To find the length of the vertical leg, we subtract the y-coordinates of M and N: $2 - (-4) = 6$ units.

We can then use the Pythagorean Theorem to solve for the length of $\overline{MN}$:

$$8^2 + 6^2 = MN^2$$

$$100 = MN^2$$

$$MN = \sqrt{100}$$

$$MN = 10$$

$\overline{MN}$ is 10 units long.

 Watch Video 3.14, Distance Using the Pythagorean Theorem, at **videos.ivyglobal.com.**

Reflections, Rotations, and Translations

A **reflection** of an object takes place when an object is "flipped" over a line. The new object will be facing the opposite direction, like a mirror image of the original object. In the coordinate plane, a line or shape can be reflected over any line or axis. In the diagrams below, look what happens when a triangle is reflected horizontally over the *y*-axis or vertically over the *x*-axis:

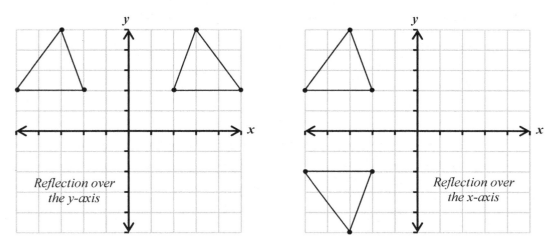

A **rotation** occurs when an object is "turned" around a point. If an object is rotated 90°, it appears to be on its side, and if it is rotated 180°, it appears to be upside-down. If an object is rotated 360°, it comes "full circle" back to its original position because there are a total of 360 degrees in a circle.

You'll need to be able to tell the difference between a rotation and a reflection. Look what happens when the triangle below is rotated 90° and 180° around the origin:

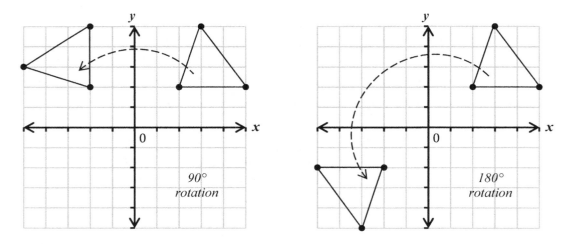

Both reflections and rotations affect the way an object faces on the coordinate plane. By contrast, a **translation** occurs when an object is "slid" into another position without changing its shape, size, or the way it faces. An object can be translated a certain number of units horizontally, vertically, or both. Look what happens when the following triangle is translated horizontally 6 units to the left and vertically 6 units down:

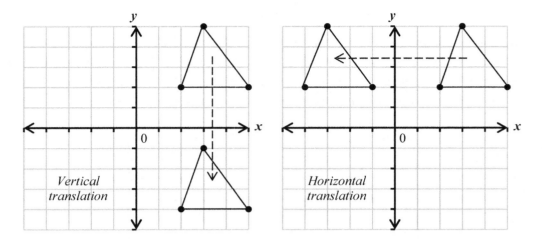

What if you need to translate an object both horizontally *and* vertically? Move each one of its points the same vertical and horizontal distance. In the diagram below, we can translate parallelogram *EFGH* six units to the right and five units up by moving each point the same distance:

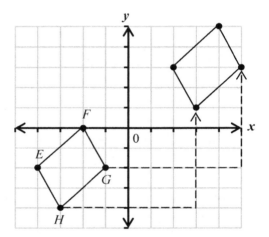

The dotted arrows show how points *G* and *H* are each moved horizontally 6 units and vertically 5 units. To complete the parallelogram, points *E* and *F* are moved in the same way.

Watch Video 3.15, Reflections, Rotations, and Translations, at **videos.ivyglobal.com.**

Practice Questions: Coordinate Geometry

For questions 1-5, refer to the diagram to the right.

1. Which of the points has an *x*-coordinate of 3?

2. Which two points have *y*-coordinates of −2?

3. Which point has the coordinates (4, −4)?

4. What are the coordinates of point *A*?

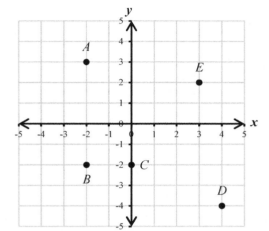

5. Erin wants to plot a point three units to the right of point *B* and five units above. What will be the coordinates of her new point?

For questions 6-10, refer to the diagram to the right.

6. Which point has coordinates (2, 5)?

7. What is the *x*-coordinate of point *R*?

8. In which quadrant is point *M* located?

9. What is the length of line segment $\overline{MN}$?

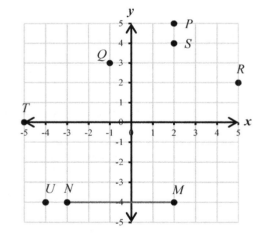

10. Georgios starts at point *Q*, and plots a new point 5 units to the right and 4 units down. What are the coordinates of his new point?

11. Mike has plotted a point located four vertical units and five horizontal units away from the origin. If this point is located in Quadrant II, what are its coordinates?

12. What is the length of line segment $\overline{GH}$ in the diagram below?

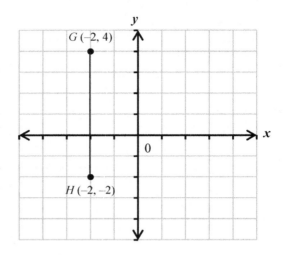

13. Sarah has drawn a line segment whose endpoints have the coordinates (2, 4) and (−2, 4). What is the length of this line segment?

14. What is the perimeter of rectangle *KLMN* in the diagram below?

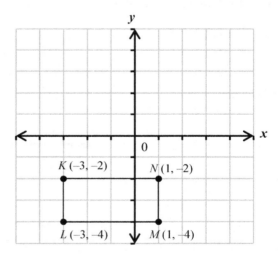

15. What is the area of the shaded triangle in the figure below?

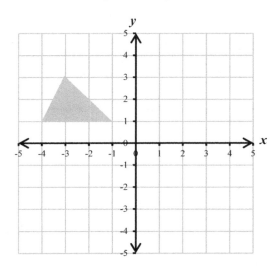

16. Consider the letters below. Which letter's reflection across the y-axis would look exactly the same is its reflection across the x-axis?

(A) **M**

(B) **H**

(C) **P**

(D) **D**

(E) **Y**

17. Which of the following figures show triangle *ABC* and its 90° rotation?

(A)
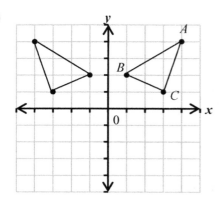

(D)
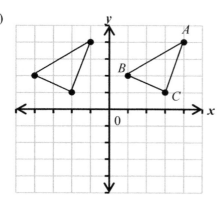

(B)
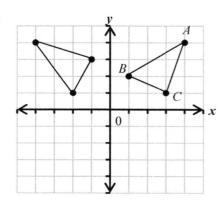

(E)
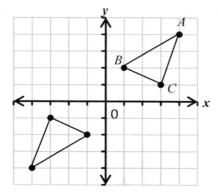

(C)
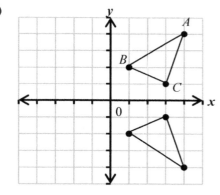

18. What is the length of line segment $\overline{RS}$ in the diagram below?

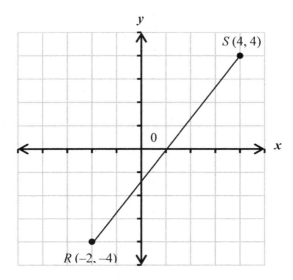

19. What is the perimeter of parallelogram *HIJK* in the diagram below?

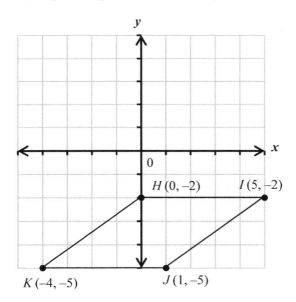

20. What is the perimeter of triangle *TUV* below?

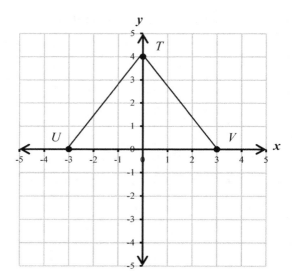

Section 6
Geometry Review

1. A 24-kilometer race is divided into three separate segments. If the first segment is 9 kilometers long and the second segment is 4 kilometers long, how long is the third segment?

   (A) 11 kilometers

   (B) 12 kilometers

   (C) 13 kilometers

   (D) 15 kilometers

   (E) 20 kilometers

2. A ranch is building a cattle corral in the shape of a regular pentagon. If each side of the corral uses 15 feet of fence, how many feet of fence will it take to build the entire corral?

   (A) 3

   (B) 15

   (C) 60

   (D) 75

   (E) 90

3. Warren started in the lower left corner of the grid to the right. He moved 6 units up, 5 units to the right, 3 units down, and 2 units to the left. Which point marks the spot where Warren landed?

   (A) Point A

   (B) Point B

   (C) Point C

   (D) Point D

   (E) Point E

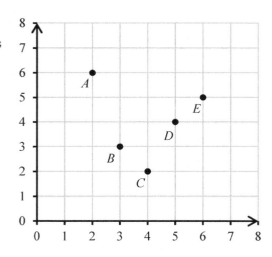

4. What is the area of a triangle that has a base of 10 cm and a height of 8 cm?

    (A) 10 cm²

    (B) 18 cm²

    (C) 20 cm²

    (D) 40 cm²

    (E) 80 cm²

5. A rectangular carpet is 12 feet wide and has an area of 84 square feet. What is the length of the carpet?

    (A) 4 ft.

    (B) 6 ft.

    (C) 7 ft.

    (D) 8 ft.

    (E) 12 ft.

6. A rectangular box is 5 feet long, 3 feet tall, and 4 feet wide. What is the total surface area of the box, in square feet?

    (A) 30

    (B) 47

    (C) 60

    (D) 94

    (E) 120

7. Noreena walked 5 blocks north, 6 blocks west, 5 blocks south, and 6 blocks east. If it took her an average of 3 minutes to walk one block, how long did her entire walk take?

    (A) 11 min.

    (B) 30 min.

    (C) 33 min.

    (D) 60 min.

    (E) 66 min.

8. What is the area, in square units, of the shaded region in the figure to the right?

    (A) 3

    (B) 4

    (C) 6

    (D) 9

    (E) 12

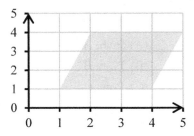

9. All of the following letters look exactly the same as their horizontal reflections EXCEPT

(A) R   (D) W

(B) I   (E) X

(C) T

10. The figure below shows three complementary angles. If angle A measures 15° and angle B measures 25°, what is the measure of the third angle?

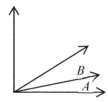

(A) 15°
(B) 25°
(C) 40°
(D) 50°
(E) 90°

11. If a rectangular sticker is 4 centimeters wide and 6 centimeters long, what is the smallest number of stickers that would completely cover a sheet of paper that measures 20 centimeters by 72 centimeters?

(A) 20
(B) 24
(C) 30
(D) 60
(E) 80

12. In the figure to the right, the image of a circle is created when a plane's propeller blade spins quickly. If the length of each propeller blade is 4 feet, what is the diameter of the circle created?

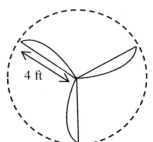

(A) 2 feet
(B) 4 feet
(C) 8 feet
(D) 12 feet
(E) 16 feet

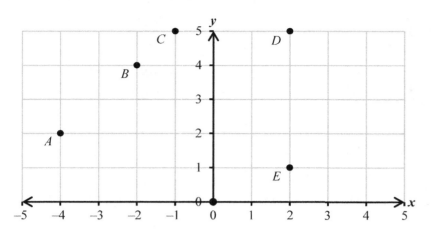

13. Which point is located at coordinates (–2, 4)?

    (A) Point A

    (B) Point B

    (C) Point C

    (D) Point D

    (E) Point E

14. What are the coordinates of point E?

    (A) (2, 1)

    (B) (1, 2)

    (C) (–1, –2)

    (D) (–2, –1)

    (E) (2, –1)

15. Which point is located the shortest distance away from point D?

    (A) Point A

    (B) Point B

    (C) Point C

    (D) Point E

    (E) It cannot be determined from the information given.

16. If the shape below were rotated 90 degrees counter-clockwise, the resulting shape would look like which of the following options?

(A)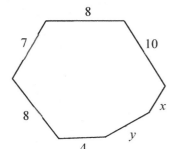

(D)

(B)

(E)

(C)

17. Kolten's fish tank holds 1200 cubic inches of water. If the tank's height is 24 inches and it width is 10 inches, what is its length?

(A) 5 inches

(B) 40 inches

(C) 120 inches

(D) 240 inches

(E) 12000 inches

18. Joe painted a wall that measured 8 feet tall and 20 feet wide. If Joe spent 20 cents on paint for every square foot of surface area, his total cost to paint this wall was

(A) $32.00

(B) $44.20

(C) $48.00

(D) $160.00

(E) $360.00

19. If the total perimeter of the polygon to the right is 48, then $x + y =$

(A) 5.5

(B) 6

(C) 11

(D) 37

(E) It cannot be determined from the information given.

20. The ceiling of a room measures 16 feet by 10 feet, and Emma wants to install a wooden border along the perimeter of the ceiling. If the wood costs 50 cents per foot, how much will Emma spend on the total length of wood necessary to border the perimeter of the ceiling?

   (A) $13
   (B) $26
   (C) $52
   (D) $80
   (E) $160

21. A cargo ship is being loaded with rectangular crates. Each crate measures 2 meters by 3 meters by 5 meters. If the ship's cargo area is 10 meters long, 30 meters wide, and 50 meters tall, how many crates will fit into the ship's cargo area?

   (A) 30
   (B) 150
   (C) 500
   (D) 800
   (E) 15000

22. In the figure below, a dog is tethered by a leash to a point on the edge of a barn. If the leash is 10 feet long, the dog will be able to reach all of the following points EXCEPT

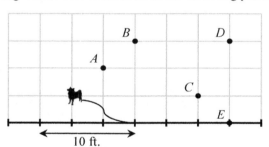

   (A) Point A
   (B) Point B
   (C) Point C
   (D) Point D
   (E) Point E

23. A rectangular block of metal is 5 inches long, 8 inches wide, and 2 inches tall. If each cubic inch of metal weighs 5 pounds, what is the total weight of the block?

    (A) 16 pounds
    (B) 40 pounds
    (C) 80 pounds
    (D) 200 pounds
    (E) 400 pounds

24. In the figure below, line segments $\overline{MP}$ and $\overline{PQ}$ both have a length of 6. If point N is the midpoint of $\overline{MP}$, what is the distance between point N and point Q?

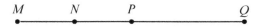

    (A) 3
    (B) 6
    (C) 9
    (D) 12
    (E) 18

25. If three angles are supplementary, which of the following could NOT be the measure of one of these angles?

    (A) 45°
    (B) 60°
    (C) 90°
    (D) 179°
    (E) 181°

26. The triangular prism to the right is 4 units tall and 8 units long. If the total volume of the prism if 96 cubic units, what is the value of x?

    (A) 4
    (B) 6
    (C) 12
    (D) 24
    (E) 32

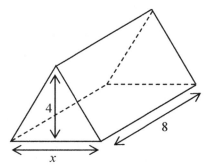

27. In the figure below, Gerry is connecting points on a grid to make a rectangle. If point L, M, and N are the first three corners of his rectangle, what will be the coordinates of the fourth corner?

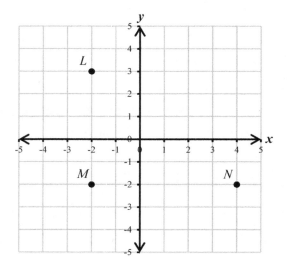

(A) $(-2, -2)$
(B) $(4, -2)$
(C) $(4, 3)$
(D) $(3, 4)$
(E) $(2, 2)$

28. In the figure below, the centers of four identical circles form the corners of a square. If the diameter of each circle is 6, what is the area of the square?

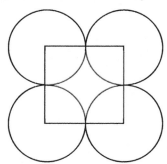

(A) 9
(B) 12
(C) 24
(D) 36
(E) 144

29. A rectangular flower bed is one fifth as long as it is wide. If the flower bed is 3 meters long, what is its area, in square meters?

   (A) 0.6
   (B) 1.5
   (C) 3.5
   (D) 36
   (E) 45

30. A container of orange juice is 10 centimeters wide, 10 centimeters long, and 20 centimeters tall. If one orange can yield 20 cubic centimeters of juice, how many oranges are needed to produce enough juice to fill the container?

   (A) 10
   (B) 100
   (C) 200
   (D) 2,000
   (E) 40,000

31. In the figure to the right, what is the value of n?

   (A) 20
   (B) 40
   (C) 50
   (D) 140
   (E) 180

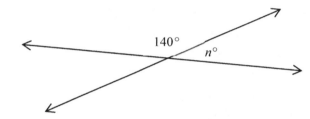

32. The circle in the figure below fits exactly inside of a square. If the radius of the circle is 4, what is the area of the square?

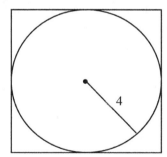

   (A) 4
   (B) 8
   (C) 16
   (D) 32
   (E) 64

33. In the figure to the right, angles *H* and *K* are complementary. If angle *H* is twice as large as angle *K*, what is the measure of angle *K*?

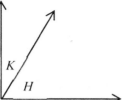

   (A) 30
   (B) 40
   (C) 60
   (D) 80
   (E) 90

34. A tank in the shape of a cube, with sides of 4 feet, is being filled with water by a hose. If the hose carries 2 cubic feet of water into the tank every second, how long will it take for the tank to be full?

   (A) 16 seconds
   (B) 32 seconds
   (C) 64 seconds
   (D) 128 seconds
   (E) 256 seconds

35. In the coordinate plane, Jia drew a line segment whose endpoints have coordinates of (4, 6) and (4, −3). How long is the line segment?

   (A) 1 unit
   (B) 2 units
   (C) 3 units
   (D) 6 units
   (E) 9 units

36. A worm is tunneling into an apple, taking the most direct path from a point on the apple's surface to the center of the apple. The apple has the shape of a sphere with a diameter of 10 centimeters. if the worm travels at a rate of 7 minutes per centimeter, how long will it take to reach the center of the apple?

   (A) 17 minutes
   (B) 35 minutes
   (C) 42 minutes
   (D) 63 minutes
   (E) 70 minutes

37. In the figure below, *ABCD* is a rectangle. If angle *AEF* measures 120° and angle *DBF* measures 50°, what is the value of *x*?

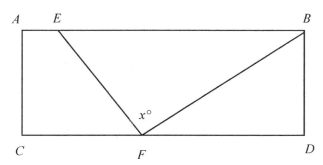

   (A) 30
   (B) 50
   (C) 60
   (D) 80
   (E) 90

38. In the figure below, a cable is connected at one end to an anchor in the ground, and at the other end to the top of a pole that is 800 feet away. If the cable is 1000 feet long, what is the height of the tower?

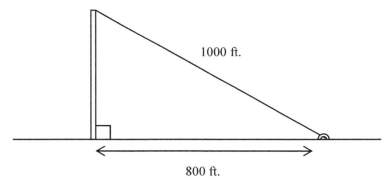

1000 ft.

800 ft.

   (A) 600 ft.
   (B) 800 ft.
   (C) 1200 ft.
   (D) 1800 ft.
   (E) 400,000 ft.

39. In the figure below, lines *r* and *s* are parallel. What is the value of *y*?

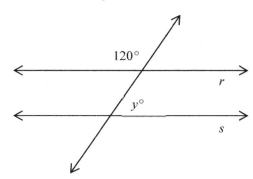

(A) 60°

(B) 70°

(C) 80°

(D) 120°

(E) 160°

40. The top of a standard hockey puck is a circle with a diameter of 6 inches. What is its area, in square inches?

(A) 3π

(B) 6π

(C) 9π

(D) 18π

(E) 36π

41. What is the length of the line segment in the figure below?

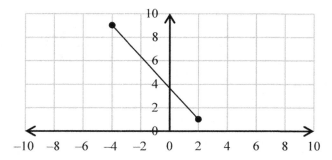

(A) 8 units

(B) 10 units

(C) 16 units

(D) 40 units

(E) 60 units

42. The right triangle in the figure below has a base of 12 and a hypotenuse of 13. What is the area of this triangle?

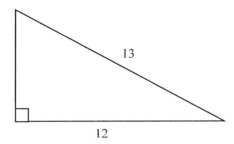

(A) 5

(B) 30

(C) 60

(D) 78

(E) 156

43. In the figure below, a rotating sprinkler sends a spray of water 4 meters long in each direction in order to water a circular area of grass. What is the area of this circle?

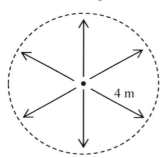

(A) 4π m^2

(B) 8π m^2

(C) 16π m^2

(D) 32π m^2

(E) 64π m^2

44. What is the perimeter of the shaded triangle in the figure to the right?

(A) 5

(B) 7

(C) 12

(D) 14

(E) 35

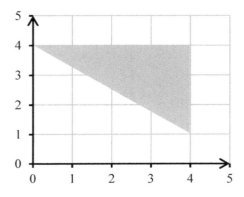

45. What is the volume, in cubic centimeters, of a cylinder with a diameter of 10 centimeters and a height of 8 centimeters?

(A) 80π

(B) 100π

(C) 160π

(D) 200π

(E) 800π

46. In the figure below, $v = 82$ and $w = 56$. What is the value of u?

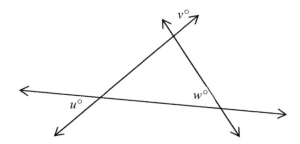

(A) 34

(B) 42

(C) 56

(D) 64

(E) 98

47. The figure below shows a circular disk rotating around its center. A point on the outside edge of this disk travels at a rate of 2π inches per second and takes 6 seconds to make a complete rotation. What is the radius of the disk, in inches?

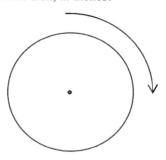

(A) 3

(B) 6

(C) 12

(D) 6π

(E) It cannot be determined from the information given.

48. A line segment drawn in the coordinate plane has one endpoint with coordinates (2, 3). If the line segment is 5 units long, which of the following could be the coordinates of its second endpoint?

(A) (2, 5)

(B) (5, 3)

(C) (0, 3)

(D) (3, 4)

(E) (6, 0)

49. If the volume of a cylinder is 400π cubic feet, and its height is 25 feet, what is its radius?

(A) 4 ft.

(B) 5 ft.

(C) 8 ft.

(D) 40 ft.

(E) 80 ft.

50. The sequence in the figure below has a diagonal of 8 cm. What is the area of the square?

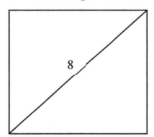

(A) 4 cm²

(B) 16 cm²

(C) 32 cm²

(D) 48 cm²

(E) 64 cm²

Data Interpretation

Section 1
Charts and Graphs

You will need to be able to analyze information presented in many different formats. When you see a diagram in the form of a chart or graph, examine it carefully to make sure you understand it. Ask yourself the following questions:

- What is the **main purpose** of this chart or graph?
- What is being compared, or what are the **variables**?
- What is the **scale**, or what **units** are being used?

Let's use these questions to analyze the chart below:

Population Growth by Town, 1960-2000			
Population (in thousands)			
Town	1960	1980	2000
Cedarville	72	83	104
Franklin	80	82	73
Pine Ridge	121	136	143

What is the **main purpose** of this chart or graph?
To answer this question, always look at the title of the chart or graph. From its title, we can tell that the chart above is meant to show the population growth of several towns from 1960 to 2000.

What is being compared, or what are the **variables**?
A variable is any category—time, place, distance, temperature, etc.—that is being measured or compared. To figure out what variables are being compared in any chart or graph, look closely at the data labels found on each column, row, or axis. The labels in the chart above tell us that our variables

for this chart include towns, dates, and populations. To be specific, we are comparing the population of three different towns (Cedarville, Franklin, and Pine Ridge) at three different dates (1960, 1980, and 2000).

What is the **scale**, or what **units** are being used?

Read very carefully any information given about scale or units in order to understand how numbers on a chart or graph are being represented. In the chart above, we are told that the population data is being represented "in thousands." This information is very important—without this information, we would think that the population of Cedarville in 1960 was only 72 people instead of 72,000 people!

Now that we understand this data in chart format, let's take a look at how it might be represented in different types of graphs. The most common types of graphs include bar graphs, line graphs, and pie charts.

Bar Graphs

A **bar graph** uses bars of different lengths to visually compare different sizes of data. Like the coordinate plane, bar graphs represent data along two axes: the x-axis is horizontal and frequently displays the labels of the variables for each bar, and the y-axis is vertical and frequently displays the amounts being measured. However, sometimes a bar graph might be displayed "sideways," so the variables are on the x-axis and the amounts being measured are on the y-axis. Pay close attention to the labels on each axis so you can determine how the information is being displayed. If a bar graph uses differently colored or patterned bars, a legend explains what other variables these colors or patterns represent.

Bar graphs are useful for comparing data across related items in the same category, or for comparing data over different time periods. Because it compares the population of similar items (towns) over different time periods, the data from the chart on the previous page can be easily represented in the following bar graph:

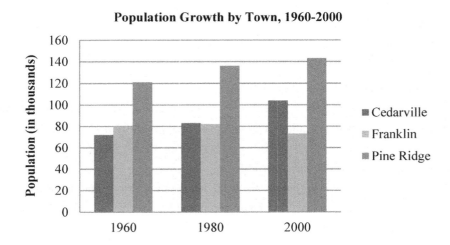

In this graph, the legend tells us that the different-colored bars represent different towns. For easy comparison, these are grouped together at each date along the *x*-axis. The *y*-axis displays what is being measured—population—and again we are told that the units are in thousands of people.

We can use this information to interpret the scale of the *y*-axis and make conclusions about data. Because numbers are given in thousands, each tick mark along the *y*-axis represents 20,000 people. Referencing these tick marks, we can tell that the population of Pine Ridge in 1960 was about 120,000, and by 1980 it had grown by about 15,000. We can also tell that the populations of Cedarville and Franklin were relatively similar in 1960 and 1980, but diverged by close to 30,000 in 2000.

Line Graphs

A **line graph** uses a line or several lines plotted against two axes to visually represent changes in amounts over time. The horizontal *x*-axis displays different dates or time periods, and the vertical *y*-axis displays the amounts being measured. If a line graph uses differently colored or patterned lines, a legend explains what variables these colors or patterns represent.

Here is how our population data would be represented on a line graph:

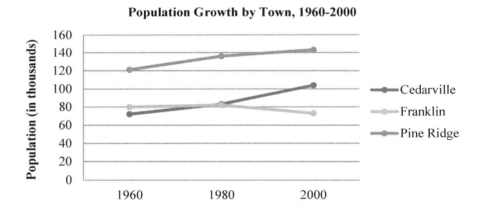

The legend tells us that each line on this graph represents a different town. Our three dates (1960, 1980, and 2000) are spaced out evenly along the *x*-axis of the graph, and population is measured on the *y*-axis. Just like our bar graph, the scale of the *y*-axis tells us that each tick mark represents 20,000 people.

Because this graph displays a line across the whole time period we are examining, we can use the graph to make estimates about population at specific years that are not listed in our chart. For example, we don't know the exact population of Pine Ridge in 1970, but by looking at the middle of the line drawn from 1960 to 1980, we can estimate that the population was around 130,000.

We can also use a line graph to determine how quickly amounts are changing over a particular time period. The **slope** of a line segment, or how steeply it is going upwards or downwards, tells us the rate of change between two points. A line going upwards means amounts are increasing, and a line going downwards means amounts are decreasing. A steep slope means amounts are increasing or decreasing quickly, and a less steep slope means amounts are changing slowly. An entirely flat (horizontal) line segment means there is no change in amount at all between the two data points.

In our graph, the line segment representing the population of Franklin between 1960 and 1980 looks pretty flat because the population of Franklin didn't change very much between 1960 and 1980. However, the line segment between 1980 and 2000 has a much steeper downward slope because the population of Franklin between those two dates changed a lot more, and it decreased. The line for Pine Ridge has an upward slope over the whole time period because the population of Pine Ridge kept increasing. However, the line is steeper from 1960 to 1980 than it is from 1980 to 2000. This means that the population of Pine Ridge increased more quickly from 1960 to 1980, and less quickly from 1980 to 2000.

Pie Charts

A **pie chart** compares amounts as percentages of a whole. Unlike a bar or line graph, a pie chart does not use axes to show changes over time. Instead, a pie chart uses a circle to represent the total amount, and appropriately sized sections of that circle to represent portions of the whole. These sections look like pieces of pie, which is why this type of graph is called a "pie chart." A legend or labels on the chart explain what data each section represents.

Because our population growth data changes over time and pie charts don't show changes over time, we can't represent all of our population data in a single pie chart. However, we can use a pie chart to show how the population of each town compares to the total population of all three towns at one point in time.

Let's look at the populations of Cedarville, Franklin, and Pine Ridge in 1980. Looking back at our table, we can find the total population of all three towns in 1980 by adding together their individual populations: 83,000 + 82,000 + 136,000 = 301,000. The following pie chart shows each town's individual population in 1980 as a percentage of this total:

Population Breakdown by Town in 1980

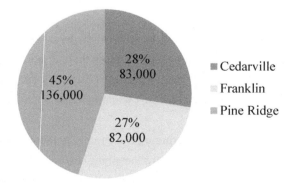

The title of this graph tells us that we are looking at population in 1980, and the legend tells us that each of the slices in this pie chart represents a town. The entire pie chart represents the total population of all three towns. From the labels and the size of these slices, we can tell that 28% of the people in these three towns lived in Cedarville, 27% lived in Franklin, and 45% lived in Pine Ridge in 1980. The data labels for each slice also tell us exactly how many people lived in each town, but this information is not always given in a pie chart.

 Watch Video 4.1, Charts and Graphs, at **videos.ivyglobal.com.**

For questions 1-2, refer to the graph below.

Survey of 200 Students' Favorite Sports

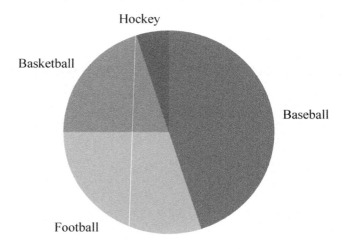

1. According to the chart, about 25% of the total group of students liked which two sports combined?

2. Approximately how many students liked either baseball or football?

For questions 3-6, refer to the chart below.

Jennifer's Cookie Sales for the Band Fundraiser		
Type of Cookie	**Price per Box**	**Number of Boxes Sold**
Chocolate Chip	$2.40	10
Peanut Butter	$2.50	8
Oatmeal Raisin	$3.00	8
Shortbread	$3.20	6

3. How many total boxes of cookies did Jennifer sell?

4. How much more money did Jennifer make by selling oatmeal raisin cookies than by selling peanut butter cookies?

5. Jennifer made exactly the same amount of money by selling which two types of cookies?

6. If Jennifer's goal was to make $100 for the school fundraiser, what is the least number of additional boxes of cookies that she would have to sell?

For questions 7-10, refer to the graph below.

Breakdown of Cottonwood High School's $360 Budget for the Spring Dance

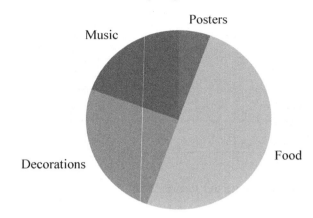

7. About what percent of the budget is devoted to decorations for the Spring Dance?

8. About how much money is Cottonwood High School spending on food for the Spring Dance?

9. Cottonwood High School has budgeted the same amount for decorations as for what other two categories combined?

10. If Cottonwood High School decided to eliminate funding for posters and divide its total budget evenly among food, music, and decorations, approximately how much more money would it spend on decorations?

For questions 11-14, refer to the graph below.

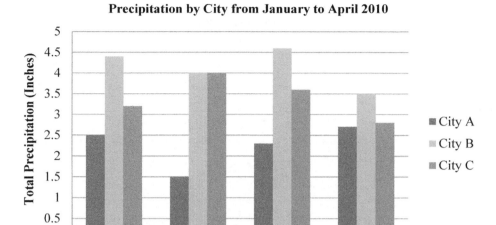

11. In which month did City B and City C experience the same amount of precipitation?

12. Which city's precipitation increased between January and February?

13. In which month did City B experience about twice as much precipitation as City A?

14. Over all four months, about how much greater was the total precipitation of City C than the total precipitation of City A?

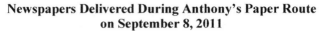

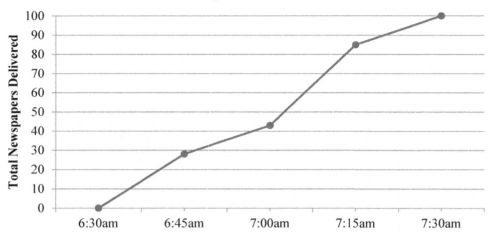

15. How many total newspapers did Anthony deliver on the morning of September 8, 2011?

16. About how many newspapers did Anthony deliver between 7:15 and 7:30am?

17. Over what 15-minute time period did Anthony deliver newspapers at the fastest rate?

18. Was Anthony's overall delivery rate faster during the first half or the second half of his paper route?

For questions 19-20, refer to the chart below.

Highway Repair Costs by County in 2011		
County	Highway Repair Costs	Miles of Highway in County
Pinellas	$45,000	300
Hillsborough	$169,000	1,300
Glendale	$81,000	450

19. According to the chart above, which county had the highest repair costs per mile of highway in 2011?

20. Pinellas County wants to reduce the amount of money it spends repairing each mile of highway. If Pinellas County could have repaired its highways at the same repair cost per mile as Hillsborough County, how much money would Pinellas County have saved in 2011?

Section 2
Range, Mean, Median, and Mode

In order to draw conclusions about sets of data, you will need to know how to determine the range, mean, median, and mode. Let's look at the definitions for these concepts and how to use them.

Ranges

The **range** of a set of data is the difference between the biggest and smallest values. The range tells you the interval where all of the data occurs. To find the range of any set of data, put the data in numerical order and subtract the smallest from the biggest value.

Example

Find the range of Adam's quiz scores in the chart below.

Adam's History Quiz Scores				
Quiz 1	**Quiz 2**	**Quiz 3**	**Quiz 4**	**Quiz 5**
83	87	90	87	94

This chart shows a student's scores on five history quizzes. To find the range of these scores, let's first put them in numerical order:

$$83, 87, 87, 90, 94$$

Adam's lowest score was 83 and his highest was 94, so his range is the difference between these two:

$$\text{Range} = 94 - 83 = 11$$

Adam's scores fall within a range of 11 points.

Mean (Average)

The **mean** of a set of data is the same thing as its **average**. We often hear the word "average" in phrases like "the average student" or "the average family," when we want to talk about characteristics similar to a lot of different students or families. It is important to remember that an average is just a way of summarizing a lot of different points of data, but it might not actually exist in real life. For example, we might be told that the average family in a country has 2.5 people. Of course this is impossible—there is no such thing as a half of a person! This means that most of the families surveyed may have had either 2 or 3 people, and the best way of summarizing the data is to say that the "average" family is halfway in between 2 and 3 people.

To calculate the mean or average of a set of data, add up all of the data and divide by the total number of values:

$$\text{Average} = \frac{\text{Sum of data}}{\text{Total number of values}}$$

For example, consider the table on the previous page:

Example	

What is the average of Adam's quiz scores in the previous chart?

To calculate the average, we would find the sum of all of his quiz scores and then divide by the total number of scores (5):

$$\text{Average} = \frac{83 + 87 + 90 + 87 + 94}{5} = \frac{441}{5} = 88.2$$

According to this formula, Adam's average quiz score was 88.2. Adam didn't actually score 88.2 on any quiz, but his scores center around this number.

Some questions may ask you to work backwards and find a certain piece of information based on an average that is provided. For these types of questions, you will need to use the formula above and a little bit of algebra to solve for a missing number.

For example, consider the chart on the previous page again:

Example	

Adam has one more history quiz coming up, and he would like to raise his average to 90. What would he need to score on the next quiz in order to raise his average from 88.2?

We know that his average is equal to the sum of all of his scores divided by the total number of scores, and with one extra quiz, the total number would be 6. For his average to equal 90, the sum of his scores would have to be equal to 90 multiplied by 6:

$$\frac{\text{Sum of scores}}{6} = 90$$

$$\text{Sum of scores} = 90 \times 6$$

$$\text{Sum of scores} = 540$$

The sum of Adam's scores after he takes his sixth quiz needs to be 540. Therefore, we can subtract all of his other scores from 540 to find what his sixth score needs to be:

$$\text{Sixth score} = 540 - (83 + 87 + 90 + 87 + 94) = 99$$

Adam would need to score a 99 on his sixth history quiz in order to raise his average from 88.2 to 90.

Median

The **median** refers to the value that is exactly in the middle of a set of data. The median is another way of summarizing your data, but it is often a different number than the average. To find the median, put all of the data in numerical order and locate the middle number.

Example

What is the median of Adam's five history quiz scores in the previous chart?

To solve the problem, we would put Adam's quiz scores in numerical order:

$$83, 87, 87, 90, 94$$

The middle number in this data set is 87, so Adam's median history quiz score is 87.

What if your data set has an even number of values, so there is no middle number? In this case, the median is the average of the two numbers closest to the middle. Go through the same process to put the data in numerical order and find the two numbers closest to the middle. Then, take their average by adding them together and dividing by two.

Example

If Adam is able to score a 99 on his sixth history quiz, what will his new median score be?

If Adam manages to score a 99, the data for his scores will be as follows:

$$83, 87, 87, 90, 94, 99$$

There is no number in the middle of this set of data, but the two numbers closest to the middle are 87 and 90. To find the median of this set of data, take the average of these two numbers:

$$\frac{87 + 90}{2} = 88.5$$

The average of 87 and 90 is 88.5, so 88.5 would be the median of Adam's six history quiz scores.

Mode

The **mode** of a set of data refers to the value that occurs most frequently. A set of data may have one or more modes if there are one or more numbers that occur more frequently than any other number. A set of data may have no mode if all values occur the same number of times.

Example

What is the mode of Adam's history quiz scores in the previous chart?

In Adam's history quiz scores, the number 87 occurs twice. There is no other number that occurs more than once in this set of data, so 87 is the mode.

Example

Here are all of the scores that Adam and his classmates received on their last history quiz: 91, 88, 94, 90, 82, 79, 84, 94, 85, 88, 93, 97, 92, 80, 96. Does this set of data have a mode or modes? If so, identify the mode or modes.

The answer to this question is easiest to find out if we put the data in numerical order:

$$79, 80, 82, 84, 85, \boxed{88, 88,} 90, 91, 92, 93, \boxed{94, 94,} 96, 97$$

Both 88 and 94 occur two times, and the rest of the values only occur once. Therefore, 88 and 94 are the two modes of these quiz scores.

Watch Video 4.2, Range, Mean, Median, and Mode, at **videos.ivyglobal.com.**

Practice Questions: Range, Mean, Median, and Mode

For questions 1-4, refer to the chart below.

Sarah's Snack and Coffee Purchases				
Monday	**Tuesday**	**Wednesday**	**Thursday**	**Friday**
$2.50	$1.20	$4.00	$1.20	$3.10

1. What is the range of this set of data?

2. What is the median of this set of data?

3. On average, how much did Sarah spend per day on snacks and coffee?

4. Does this set of data have a mode or modes? If so, identify the mode or modes:

For questions 5-9, refer to the data below.

To train for a race, Marion is timing herself during her 10-kilometer practice runs. Here are her times (in minutes) for her last 6 runs:

$$53, 51, 52.5, 50, 49.5, 50$$

5. What is the range of Marion's practice times?

6. What was her average time?

7. What was her median time?

8. Does this set of data have a mode or modes? If so, identify the mode or modes:

9. Marion just logged the time for her seventh practice run and re-calculated her median time with this new piece of data. To her surprise, she discovered that her median time remained exactly the same as before. If this is true, what was the time for her seventh practice run?

For questions 10-13, refer to the graph below.

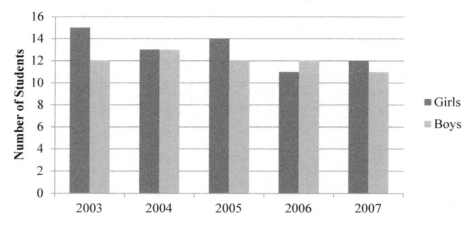

Size of Mrs. White's 6th Grade Class, 2003-2007

10. What was the median number of boys in Mrs. White's class from 2003 to 2007?

11. What was the average number of students in Mrs. White's class from 2003 to 2007?

12. What was the range of Mrs. White's total class size from 2003 to 2007?

13. On average, how many more girls than boys were in Mrs. White's class each year?

14. If the average of four numbers is 12, what is the sum of these four numbers?

15. Jordan's class can win a pizza party if each student reads an average of 5 books over the period of a month. So far, the 24 students in Jordan's class have read a total of 96 books. How many more books, on average, does each student need to read in order for the class to win a pizza party?

16. Allen scored an average of 91 on five algebra tests. If his first four test scores were 92, 90, 86, and 88, what did he score on his fifth test?

17. The sum of three consecutive even integers is 18. What is the median of these three integers?

18. Elisa has a summer job at a bicycle store. In June and July, she sold an average of $680 per month in bicycles and equipment. If she would like to bring her monthly average up to $700 by the end of the summer, how many dollars of bicycles and equipment does she need to sell in August?

19. A set of five numbers had an average of 14. When two of these numbers were removed, the remaining three numbers had an average of 13. What was the sum of the two numbers that were removed?

20. Jenny's family has 4 children, and Jenny is the second youngest. Each child in Jenny's family was born at least two years apart from any other child. If the median age of Jenny and her siblings is exactly 12, and her oldest sibling is 15 years old, how old is Jenny?

Section 3
Probability

Probability refers to the likelihood, or the "odds," that something will happen. Scientists and mathematicians can make educated predictions about the future by analyzing a lot of data and using the principles of probability. For example, weather forecasters use probability to predict the chance of rain tomorrow, and medical researchers use probability to predict people's chances of developing heart disease or lung cancer.

To calculate probability, use the formula below:

$$\text{Probability} = \frac{\text{Number of ways to get a specified outcome}}{\text{Number of possible outcomes}}$$

Example

What is the probability of rolling an even number on a six-sided die, which has the numbers 1 through 6?

Unless the die or the surface we are rolling on has been tampered with, there is an equal chance that we will roll any of the numbers from 1 through 6. Therefore, there are six possible outcomes. However, our specified outcome is rolling an even number, and there are only three even numbers that we can roll: 2, 4, and 6. To find the probability of rolling an even number, we divide the number of specified outcomes (3) by the number of possible outcomes (6):

$$\text{Probability of rolling an even number} = \frac{3}{6} = \frac{1}{2}$$

The probability of rolling an even number is ½. We can also state this as a decimal (0.5) or as a percent (50%). We can say that there is a "50% chance" of rolling an even number.

Our predicted probabilities do not always exactly match up with reality, particularly if we only have a small amount of data. For example, suppose you wanted to test out the probability of rolling an even number by doing an experiment. You get an evenly weighted six-sided die with numbers 1 through 6 and begin rolling the die on a flat, even surface. Based on your calculations, you would expect to roll an even number 50% of the time. At the beginning of your experiment, you might find that this is not true; after four rolls of the die, maybe only one of them gave you an even number, or maybe three of them did. However, as you continue rolling the die and accumulating more data, you should find that the percent of even numbers showing up begins to get closer and closer to 50%. It might never reach exactly 50%, but as long as it is close, you know your prediction worked for this experiment. If it doesn't get close to 50%, you know there was something wrong with either your prediction or the way you conducted the experiment.

Probabilities of Zero or One

Most probabilities will be fractions or decimals between 0 and 1, or a percent between 0% and 100%. The lower the probability, the less likely an event is to occur. The higher the probability, the more likely an event is to occur.

A probability of 0 or 0% means an event is impossible and will absolutely never occur. For instance:

Example

What is the probability of rolling the number 7 on a six-sided die, with numbers 1 through 6?

There are six possible outcomes, but the die does not have the number 7. Therefore, there are zero ways to get our specified outcome. If we plug this into our formula, we get:

$$\text{Probability of rolling the number 7} = \frac{0}{6} = 0$$

The probability of rolling the number 7 is 0, so there is a 0% chance that we will roll a 7. This event is impossible.

On the other hand, a probability of 1 or 100% means that an event is absolutely certain to happen. For instance:

Example

What is the probability of rolling a positive number on a six-sided die, with numbers 1 through 6?

There are six possible outcomes, and all six of these numbers are positive. Therefore, there are also six ways to get our specified outcome:

$$\text{Probability of rolling a positive number} = \frac{6}{6} = 1$$

The probability of rolling a positive number is 1, so there is a 100% chance that we will roll a positive number. This event is absolutely certain to happen.

Because a probability of 1 means an event is absolutely certain, you will never get a probability greater than 1 or 100%. You might hear someone say that they are "200% certain" that something is going to happen, but this is just an exaggeration—in the language of mathematics, 100% certain is the most you can be!

 Watch Video 4.3, Intro to Probability, at **videos.ivyglobal.com.**

Addition and Subtraction with Probability

Two events are **mutually exclusive** if it is impossible for both of them to happen at the same time. For example, if you roll one die, it is impossible to roll both the number 5 and the number 3. You can either roll one number or the other.

You can find the chance of one event *or* another event occurring by adding together their individual probabilities. For example:

Example

What is the probability of rolling either the number 5 or the number 3 on a six-sided die, with numbers 1 through 6?

The probability of rolling the number 5 on a six sided die is $\frac{1}{6}$ and the probability of rolling the number 3 is also $\frac{1}{6}$. To find your chances of rolling the number 5 *or* the number 3, add their probabilities together:

$$\text{Probability of rolling 5 or 3} = \frac{1}{6} + \frac{1}{6} = \frac{1}{3}$$

There is a $\frac{1}{3}$ chance that you will roll either the number 5 or the number 3.

As we learned in the section above, 1 is the greatest possible probability. If you add together the probabilities of all of the different outcomes of an event, you will get the number 1. For example:

Example

What is the probability of rolling the numbers 1, 2, 3, 4, 5, or 6 on a six-sided die?

If you roll a six sided die, you have six possible outcomes: the numbers 1, 2, 3, 4, 5, and 6. You have a $\frac{1}{6}$ chance of rolling any of these numbers. If you add all their probabilities together, you will get the number 1:

$$\text{Probability of rolling 1, 2, 3, 4, 5, or 6} = \frac{1}{6} + \frac{1}{6} + \frac{1}{6} + \frac{1}{6} + \frac{1}{6} + \frac{1}{6} = 1$$

You have a 100% probability of rolling the number 1, 2, 3, 4, 5 or 6 because there are no other options!

To find the probability that something will not happen is the same thing as finding the probability of all of the other possible outcomes. The probabilities of all of the different possible outcomes of any event will add up to 1. Therefore, the probability that something will *not* happen is 1 minus the probability that it *will* happen. For example:

Example

What is the probability of not rolling the number 4 on a six-sided die?

You have a $\frac{1}{6}$ chance of rolling the number 4 on a six-sided die. To find your chance of *not* rolling the number 4, subtract $\frac{1}{6}$ from 1:

$$\text{Probability of not rolling 4} = 1 - \frac{1}{6} = \frac{5}{6}$$

You have a $\frac{5}{6}$ chance of not rolling the number 4, but rolling any of the other possible numbers (1, 2, 3, 5, or 6).

Multiplication with Probability

If two events are **independent**, they might be able to happen at the same time, but the first event does not affect the probability of the second event. For instance, if you were to roll two dice, your chance of rolling an even number on one die does not affect your chance of rolling an even number on the second die. For each die, you still have a $\frac{1}{2}$ probability of rolling an even number.

If two events are independent, you can find the chance of *both* occurring at the same time by multiplying together their individual probabilities. For example:

Example

What is the probability of rolling two even numbers on one roll of two dice?

The probability of rolling an even number for the first die is $\frac{1}{2}$, and the probability of rolling an even number on the second die is also $\frac{1}{2}$. Simply multiply these together:

$$\text{Probability of rolling an even number on both dice} = \frac{1}{2} \times \frac{1}{2} = \frac{1}{4}$$

You have a $\frac{1}{4}$ or 25% chance of rolling an even number on both dice.

 Watch Video 4.4, Operations with Probabilities, at **videos.ivyglobal.com.**

Dependent Events: Upper Level Only

Two events are **dependent** if one event affects the probability of the other event occurring. If two events are dependent, we need to figure out what happens to the second event after the first one has taken place. For example:

Example

Janice picked cards randomly from a standard 52-card deck. She picked her first card and then set it aside, without replacing it, before drawing her second card. What is the probability that both cards were kings?

The probability for the first card is easy: there are 52 cards in the deck and 4 of them are kings, so Janice has a $\frac{4}{52}$ or $\frac{1}{13}$ chance of picking a king for her first card.

However, now that she has removed one card, the number of cards in the deck has changed. She now has only 51 cards in her deck. If her first card was a king, there are only 3 kings left. Therefore, the probability that her second card will also be a king is only $\frac{3}{51}$ or $\frac{1}{17}$.

You've figured out the probability of the first event, and how the probability of the second event will be affected if the first event takes place. You can now multiply these probabilities together to find the odds of both events occurring:

$$\text{Probability of picking two kings} = \frac{1}{13} \times \frac{3}{51} = \frac{3}{663} = \frac{1}{221}$$

If Janice is drawing two cards one at a time, without putting her first card back in the deck, the chance that she will pick two kings is 1 out of 221.

 Watch Video 4.5, Probability of Dependent Events, at **videos.ivyglobal.com.**

Probability and Geometry

You may need to use your knowledge of geometry to calculate the probability of something randomly occurring in a specific region of a geometric figure. In this case, the "number of ways to get a specified outcome" is equal to the area of the specific region, and the "number of possible outcomes" is equal to the area of the whole figure:

$$\text{Probability of something happening in a region} = \frac{\text{Area of specific region}}{\text{Area of whole figure}}$$

Example

The following diagram shows a square board with a shaded square in the middle. The board has a side length of 10 inches, and the square in the middle has a side length of 5 inches. What is the chance that a small coin thrown completely at random onto the board will land in the shaded region?

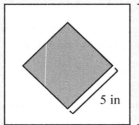

To find the probability that a randomly thrown coin will land in the shaded square, we need to find the area of the shaded square and then divide by the area of the whole figure. The shaded square has a side length of 5 inches, so its area is 25 square inches. The whole board is a square with a side length of 10 inches, so its area is 100 square inches. Therefore, the probability of our coin landing in the shaded region is:

$$\text{Probability of landing in the shaded region} = \frac{25}{100} = \frac{1}{4}$$

There is a $\frac{1}{4}$ or 25% chance that our coin, thrown truly at random, will land in the shaded square.

 Watch Video 4.6, Probability and Geometry, at **videos.ivyglobal.com.**

Practice Questions: Probability

Unless the instructions say otherwise, write all probabilities as fractions in lowest terms.

1. Mr. Johnson's class has 12 boys and 14 girls. If Mr. Johnson picks one student at random from the class, what is the probability that he will pick a boy?

2. Lisa has 2 black headbands, 1 red headband, and 1 silver headband. If she picks a headband at random, what is the probability that it will be red?

3. Shannon picks one day randomly out of the days of the week. What is the probability that she will pick a day that ends in the letter "y"?

4. The local pet store has 6 black fish and 9 red fish. If Manuel randomly chooses one fish from the pet store, what is the probability that he will choose a red fish?

5. A bakery sells chocolate, cinnamon, maple, honey, and jelly donuts. It currently has 48 total donuts in stock. If Xiwen picks one donut from the bakery at random, she has a 25% chance of picking a chocolate donut. How many chocolate donuts does the bakery have in stock?

6. Ariel and Trevor are entering a raffle to raise money for the school library. Ariel buys three tickets, and Trevor buys five tickets. At the end of the raffle, 240 tickets have been sold, and one ticket is randomly chosen as the winner. What is the probability that either Ariel or Trevor has bought the winning ticket?

7. A box of paperclips has 4 blue, 5 red, 3 green, and 3 white paperclips. If Adam chooses a paperclip randomly from the box, what is the probability that it will not be red?

8. A jar has 30 red candies, 20 blue candies, 40 green candies, and 10 yellow candies. Of the green candies, half are apple-flavored and half are lime-flavored. If Anisha picks one candy randomly from the jar, what is the probability that she will not pick a green lime-flavored candy?

For questions 9-12, refer to the figure below. The figure shows the spinner of a board game, which has four equally sized sections in the colors red, orange, pink, and yellow.

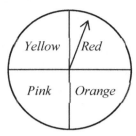

9. If the spinner is spun at random, what is the probability that it will land on red or yellow?

10. What is the probability that the spinner will not land on orange?

11. What is the probability that the spinner will land on green?

12. If the spinner is spun twice, what is the probability that it will land on pink both times?

13. In the figure below, a rectangular game board 50 centimeters long and 40 centimeters tall has two square holes, each with a side length of 10 centimeters. If a player tosses a small bean bag randomly at the board, the beanbag will either hit the game board or go through one of the holes. What is the probability that it will go through one of the holes?

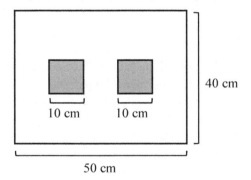

14. Jake has a six-sided die with numbers 1 through 6. If he rolls the die twice, what is the probability that he will roll two numbers whose sum is 12?

15. A standard deck of cards has 4 kings, 4 queens, 4 jacks, and 40 other cards. If Carol picks a card at random from this standard deck, what is the probability that she will pick a king, queen, or jack?

Questions 16-20 are Upper Level Only

16. In the United States, about 40% of people will be diagnosed with some type of cancer at some point in their lifetime. If two people are randomly chosen, what is the probability that both of them will be diagnosed with cancer at some point in their lifetime? Write your answer as a percent.

17. Jonas has four blue socks, ten black socks, and six white socks. If he picks two socks randomly, one at a time, without putting either sock back, what is the probability that he will pick two blue socks?

18. Kimberly has 4 six-sided dice, each with numbers 1 through 6. If she rolls all 4 dice at the same time, what is the probability that she will roll either a 1 or a 2 with each die?

19. Mrs. Chang's soccer team has 9 girls and 9 boys. In order to determine which two players will bring snacks to the first practice, Mrs. Chang picks one person randomly from the team and then picks a second person from the remaining players. What is the probability that she will pick two girls?

20. In the figure below, a circular target is made up of three concentric circles: one large circle, one medium circle, and one "bull's-eye" in the center. The radius of each concentric circle is twice as large as the radius of the next smallest circle, and the total diameter of the target is 16 inches. An arrow was shot at random and landed somewhere on the target. What is the probability that it landed on the shaded "bull's-eye" in the center?

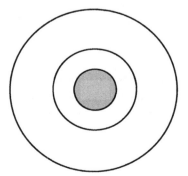

Section 4
Data Interpretation Review

For questions 1-2, refer to the graph below.

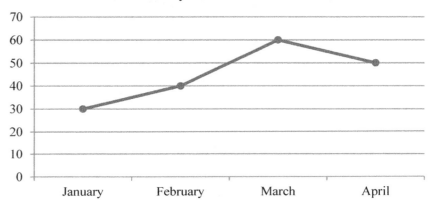

Total Books Read by Students in Mr. Graham's Class

1. Mr. Graham's students read how many more books in March than in January?

    (A) 10

    (B) 20

    (C) 30

    (D) 40

    (E) 60

2. What was the total number of books read by Mr. Graham's students from January through April?

    (A) 30

    (B) 50

    (C) 60

    (D) 120

    (E) 180

For questions 3-4, refer to the graph below.

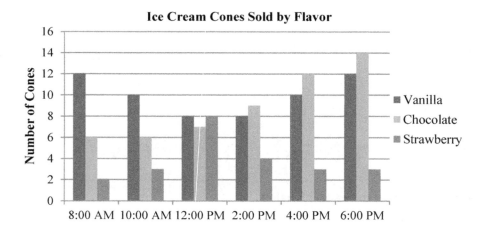

3. How many more total ice cream cones were sold at 6PM than at 12PM?

    (A) 3

    (B) 4

    (C) 5

    (D) 6

    (E) 7

4. How many more vanilla ice cream cones than chocolate ice cream cones were sold throughout the entire day?

    (A) 5

    (B) 6

    (C) 7

    (D) 8

    (E) 9

5. A bag contains 6 red markers, 9 yellow markers, 4 blue markers, and 5 green markers. If Pooja randomly picks a marker from the bag, what is the probability that she will pick a red marker?

    (A) $\dfrac{1}{24}$

    (B) $\dfrac{1}{6}$

    (C) $\dfrac{1}{4}$

    (D) $\dfrac{1}{3}$

    (E) $\dfrac{2}{3}$

For questions 6-7, refer to the graph below.

Pets Owned by 800 Students

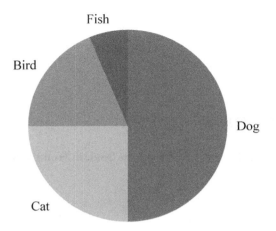

6. About how many students own either a bird or a fish?

    (A) 150
    (B) 200
    (C) 300
    (D) 400
    (E) 600

7. If one of the students were selected at random, what is the probability that he or she would own a dog?

    (A) 10%
    (B) 20%
    (C) 25%
    (D) 33%
    (E) 50%

8. In English class, Julia has received scores of 87, 84, 75, and 90 on her first four quizzes. What is the median of Julia's quiz scores?

    (A) 15
    (B) 75
    (C) 84
    (D) 85.5
    (E) 87.5

9. A box has 30 multi-colored jellybeans. If Eric randomly chooses a jellybean from the box, he has a 50% chance of choosing a blue jellybean. How many blue jellybeans are in the box?

(A) 3

(B) 5

(C) 6

(D) 10

(E) 15

For questions 10-11, refer to the graph below.

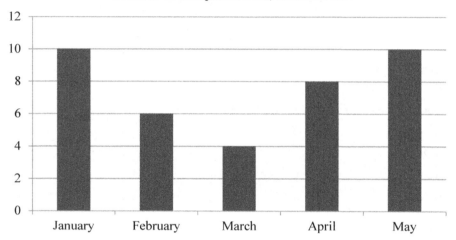

Number of Computers Sold, in Hundreds

10. How many fewer computers were sold in March than in January?

(A) 4

(B) 6

(C) 10

(D) 400

(E) 600

11. The number of computers sold in May was how many times the number of computers sold in March?

(A) 2.5

(B) 4

(C) 10

(D) 600

(E) 1,000

12. If Jack rolls one regular six-sided die, he has an equal chance of rolling any number from 1 through 6. What is the probability that he will roll a number less than 3?

(A) $\frac{1}{6}$

(B) $\frac{1}{3}$

(C) $\frac{1}{2}$

(D) $\frac{2}{3}$

(E) $\frac{5}{6}$

For question 13, refer to the graph below.

Eye Color of a Group of Students

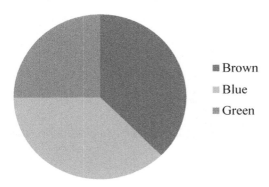

■ Brown
■ Blue
■ Green

13. If there were 900 students in the group depicted in the graph above, about how many had green eyes?

(A) 150

(B) 225

(C) 300

(D) 350

(E) 450

14. If the largest of seven consecutive integers is 18, what is the average of the seven integers?

(A) 12

(B) 15

(C) 16

(D) 17

(E) 18

For questions 15-16, refer to the graph below.

Number of Laps Run in Gym Class

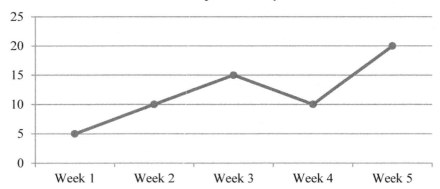

15. During the time period in the graph above, what was the average number of laps run in gym class each week?

(A) 8

(B) 10

(C) 12

(D) 15

(E) 20

16. What was the median number of laps run in gym class during the time period in the graph above?

(A) 7.5

(B) 10

(C) 12

(D) 12.5

(E) 15

17. If Kyle chooses at random one month from the calendar year, what is the probability that he will choose a month whose spelling ends in the letter "y"?

(A) $\dfrac{1}{6}$

(B) $\dfrac{1}{4}$

(C) $\dfrac{1}{3}$

(D) $\dfrac{5}{12}$

(E) $\dfrac{1}{2}$

For questions 18-20, refer to the chart below.

Voter Survey by Town			
	Number of Voters		
Town	Political Party A	Political Party B	Independent
Fallsburg	121	211	80
Hillcrest	165	95	35
Railroad Junction	75	85	95

18. For the three towns in the chart above, the average number of independent voters per town is

(A) 15

(B) 55

(C) 60

(D) 70

(E) 90

19. How many more Political Party B voters live in Fallsburg than Political Party A voters who live in Hillcrest?

(A) 46

(B) 70

(C) 90

(D) 165

(E) 211

20. Across all three towns, how many more total voters would Political Party A need in order to have the same number of total voters as Political Party B?

(A) 20

(B) 30

(C) 35

(D) 45

(E) 50

For questions 21-22, refer to the graph below.

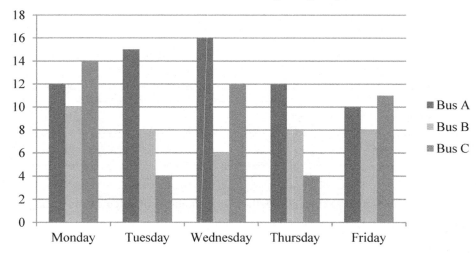

Number of Bus Passengers by Day

21. From Monday through Friday, Bus A had about how many more average passengers each day than Bus B?

    (A) 5
    (B) 8
    (C) 13
    (D) 15
    (E) 25

22. On which day of the week was there the largest difference in the number of passengers between any two of the buses?

    (A) Monday
    (B) Tuesday
    (C) Wednesday
    (D) Thursday
    (E) Friday

23. At a bicycle rental store, Colleen can choose among 10 silver bikes, 8 red bikes, and 7 blue bikes. If Colleen chooses one bike randomly, what is the probability that she does NOT choose a silver bike?

    (A) 20%
    (B) 33%
    (C) 40%
    (D) 50%
    (E) 60%

24. Five consecutive integers have a median of 23. The smallest of these integers is

(A) 18
(B) 20
(C) 21
(D) 22
(E) 25

For question 25, refer to the chart below.

Daily Clothing Sales for Weeks 1 and 2, in Dollars		
	Week 1	Week 2
Monday	$10,000	$6,000
Tuesday	$12,000	$4,000
Wednesday	$8,000	$3,000
Thursday	$14,000	$7,000
Friday	$16,000	$5,000

25. The average daily sales for Week 1 were how much greater than the average daily sales for Week 2?

(A) $5,000
(B) $7,000
(C) $10,000
(D) $12,000
(E) $16,000

26. John and Susan went apple-picking four times in September. During these four trips, John picked a total of 144 apples. If Susan picked more apples than John, what is the smallest average number of apples Susan must have picked per trip?

(A) 5
(B) 35
(C) 37
(D) 145
(E) 576

27. When Kristine rolls a standard six-sided die, she has an equal chance of rolling any number from 1 through 6. If Kristine rolls the same die 100 times, about how many times is she likely to roll a number greater than 4?

    (A) 17 times
    (B) 33 times
    (C) 40 times
    (D) 50 times
    (E) 66 times

28. A bookshelf has 3 adventure books, 2 history books, and 3 science fiction books. If Briana randomly chooses a book from the shelf, what is the probability that she will NOT choose a history book?

    (A) 12.5%
    (B) 25%
    (C) 37.5%
    (D) 62.5%
    (E) 75%

29. Team Red recently played Team Blue in a basketball game, and Team Blue lost with a score of 41 points. If 6 players played for Team Red, the average number of points scored per Team Red player must have been at least:

    (A) 5
    (B) 6
    (C) 7
    (D) 8
    (E) 9

Number of Sick Children by Illness and by School		
	Children with a Cold	Children with the Flu
School A	125	50
School B	55	30
School C	30	10

30. For each school in the chart above, the number of children with a cold is

    (A) greater than the number of children with the flu

    (B) equal to the number of children with the flu

    (C) less than the number of children with the flu

    (D) twice the number of children with the flu

    (E) three times the number of children with the flu

31. What is the average number of sick children per school across all three schools?

    (A) 20

    (B) 50

    (C) 85

    (D) 100

    (E) 300

32. If A represents the average number of slices of pizza that Adam ate each day from Monday to Friday, which expression represents the total number of pizza slices that Adam ate over that time period?

    (A) A

    (B) 5

    (C) $\dfrac{5A}{5}$

    (D) 5A

    (E) It cannot be determined from the information given.

Town Populations by Decade

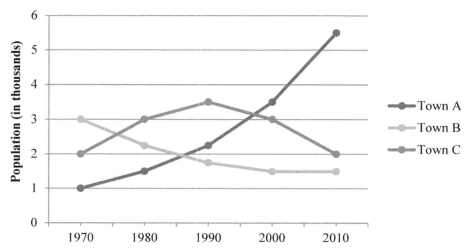

33. Between 1970 and 2010, the highest population in Town A was about how much larger than the highest population of Town B?

    (A) 2,000
    (B) 2,500
    (C) 3,000
    (D) 5,500
    (E) 25,000

34. If the population of Town C continues to decline at the same rate as it did between 2000 and 2010, in approximately which year will the town's population be zero?

    (A) 2011
    (B) 2012
    (C) 2015
    (D) 2020
    (E) 2030

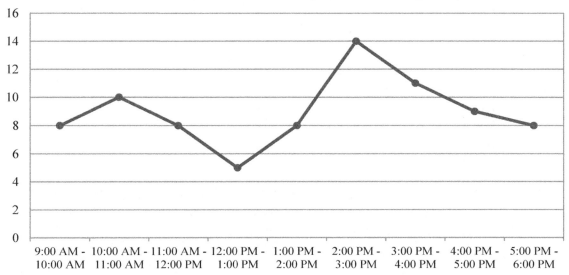

35. Over the time period in the graph above, car production increased at the fastest rate

 (A) between 9:00 AM and 10:00 AM

 (B) between 12:00 PM and 1:00 PM

 (C) between 1:00 PM and 2:00 PM

 (D) between 2:00 PM and 3:00 PM

 (E) between 4:00 PM and 5:00 PM

36. If the factory had been able to produce cars all day at its highest hourly rate, how many cars would the factory have been able to produce from 9:00AM to 6:00PM?

 (A) 14

 (B) 45

 (C) 72

 (D) 90

 (E) 126

37. While training for a swim meet, Jennifer swims four laps at the following speeds: 2:20, 2:30, 2:35, and 2:15 minutes. If Jennifer wants to keep her median lap time the same, how fast must she swim her fifth lap?

 (A) 2:15 min

 (B) 2:20 min

 (C) 2:25 min

 (D) 2:30 min

 (E) 2:35 min

38. If Elias rolls a standard six-sided die, he has an equal chance of rolling any number from 1 through 6. What is the probability that he will NOT roll either a 2 or a 6?

(A) $\dfrac{1}{36}$

(B) $\dfrac{1}{6}$

(C) $\dfrac{1}{3}$

(D) $\dfrac{2}{3}$

(E) $\dfrac{3}{4}$

39. In her first four basketball games, Jane scored 22, 26, 18, and 12 points. By the end of her fifth game, Jane's average score across all five games was 21 points per game. How many points did Jane score in her fifth basketball game?

(A) 14

(B) 21

(C) 22

(D) 27

(E) 33

40. A standard deck of 52 cards has 4 aces and 4 kings. If Jerome randomly chooses one card from a standard deck, what is the probability that he will choose either an ace or a king?

(A) $\dfrac{1}{52}$

(B) $\dfrac{1}{13}$

(C) $\dfrac{1}{8}$

(D) $\dfrac{2}{13}$

(E) $\dfrac{4}{13}$

41. On a certain math exam, the 15 students in Mr. Donaldson's class scored an average of 80. On the same exam, the 10 students in Ms. Smith's class scored an average of 90. What was the combined average score for all of the students in Mr. Donaldson's and Ms. Smith's classes?

    (A) 80
    (B) 84
    (C) 85
    (D) 86
    (E) 90

42. Three different positive integers have an average of 5. What is the largest possible value for any one of these integers?

    (A) 5
    (B) 6
    (C) 12
    (D) 13
    (E) It cannot be determined from the information given.

43. A flower shop had 3 roses, 3 tulips, and 4 carnations. John bought a rose, and then decided to buy another flower. If he randomly chose another flower from the shop's remaining selection, what is the probability that he chose a carnation?

    (A) $\dfrac{2}{5}$

    (B) $\dfrac{4}{7}$

    (C) $\dfrac{3}{9}$

    (D) $\dfrac{4}{9}$

    (E) $\dfrac{7}{10}$

44. Kim scored an average grade of 82 on her first four English quizzes. She wants to raise her average to a grade of 84. What is the lowest grade she can receive on her fifth English quiz in order to achieve this goal?

    (A) 82
    (B) 84
    (C) 88
    (D) 90
    (E) 92

45. The figure below shows a square game board with two shaded square areas. The sides of the game board are 10 inches long, and the sides of each of the shaded squares are 5 inches long. A coin was thrown at random and landed somewhere on the game board. What is the probability that it landed on one of the shaded squares?

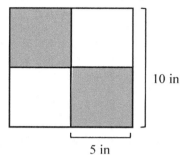

10 in

5 in

(A) 10%

(B) 20%

(C) 25%

(D) 50%

(E) 75%

Questions 46-50 are Upper Level Only.

46. When Susan rolls a regular six-sided die, she has an equal chance of rolling any number from 1 through 6. If she rolls two regular six-sided dice, what is the probability that she will roll two numbers with a sum of 7?

(A) $\frac{1}{9}$

(B) $\frac{1}{6}$

(C) $\frac{7}{36}$

(D) $\frac{1}{4}$

(E) $\frac{1}{3}$

47. A student club has 16 members: 8 boys and 8 girls. To represent the club at an upcoming event, 2 members are randomly chosen, one at a time. What is the probability that both members chosen will be girls?

(A) $\dfrac{7}{30}$

(B) $\dfrac{1}{4}$

(C) $\dfrac{7}{16}$

(D) $\dfrac{1}{2}$

(E) 1

48. Both Kate and Jim work at the Corner Ice Cream Shop. If Jim sells x ice cream cones and Kate sells $3x + 4$ ice cream cones, the average number of ice cream cones sold by each employee is equal to

(A) x

(B) $2x + 2$

(C) $2x + 4$

(D) $\dfrac{3x}{2} + 2$

(E) $\dfrac{3x}{2} + 4$

49. The figure below shows a circular board with a painted circle in the middle. The board has a total diameter of 8 inches, and the painted circle has a diameter of 4 inches. A dart was thrown at random and landed somewhere on the board. What is the probability that it landed in the painted circle?

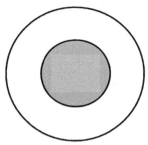

(A) 6.25%

(B) 12.5%

(C) 25%

(D) 50%

(E) 75%

50. A pond contains 4 green frogs and 3 yellow frogs. Each week, one frog is randomly selected from the pond and then returned back to the pond. What is the probability that a green frog will be selected two weeks in a row?

(A) $\dfrac{9}{49}$

(B) $\dfrac{2}{7}$

(C) $\dfrac{3}{7}$

(D) $\dfrac{4}{7}$

(E) $\dfrac{16}{49}$

Answers
Chapter 5

Arithmetic

Addition Drills Answer Key						
27 +3 **30**	13 +9 **22**	39 +2 **41**	10 +7 **17**	42 +8 **50**	75 +6 **81**	98 +7 **105**
67 +23 **90**	72 +35 **107**	18 +49 **67**	37 +14 **51**	68 +41 **109**	99 +27 **126**	32 +85 **117**
55 +12 **67**	82 +44 **126**	32 +16 **48**	63 +14 **77**	18 +99 **117**	75 +75 **150**	69 +64 **133**
78 + 98 = **176**	39 + 42 = **81**	18 + 54 = **72**	37 + 84 = **121**	28 + 18 = **46**	90 + 40 = **130**	22 + 53 = **75**
125 + 5 **130**	534 + 9 **543**	639 + 1 **640**	832 + 7 **839**	422 + 9 **431**	799 + 1 **800**	502 + 3 **505**
648 +22 **670**	331 +86 **417**	510 +27 **537**	396 +19 **415**	421 +90 **511**	307 +21 **328**	517 +17 **534**
392 +184 **576**	739 +717 **1456**	402 +184 **586**	492 +391 **883**	246 +184 **430**	582 +909 **1491**	521 +486 **1007**
329 428 +186 **943**	42 593 +204 **839**	821 12 +947 **1780**	82 194 +53 **329**	529 438 +167 **1134**	625 14 +39 **678**	527 941 +368 **1836**

Subtraction Drills Answer Key						
13 − 2 **11**	62 − 5 **57**	41 − 9 **32**	73 − 1 **72**	64 − 4 **60**	94 − 7 **87**	40 − 3 **37**
72 − 52 **20**	81 − 59 **22**	54 − 37 **17**	90 − 31 **59**	84 − 73 **11**	29 − 17 **12**	40 − 27 **13**
99 − 42 **57**	58 − 39 **19**	56 − 38 **18**	84 − 27 **57**	91 − 57 **34**	30 − 22 **8**	73 − 15 **58**
86 − 42 = **44**	72 − 65 = **7**	62 − 43 = **19**	95 − 78 = **17**	48 − 43 = **5**	81 − 72 = **9**	57 − 31 = **26**
613 − 5 **608**	749 − 7 **742**	397 − 9 **388**	942 − 3 **939**	264 − 4 **260**	481 − 9 **472**	285 − 7 **278**
849 − 31 **818**	762 − 40 **722**	492 − 32 **460**	781 − 39 **742**	267 − 69 **198**	843 − 85 **758**	328 − 57 **271**
752 − 321 **431**	481 − 278 **203**	473 − 327 **146**	849 − 212 **637**	747 − 381 **366**	604 − 518 **86**	582 − 175 **407**
391 286 − 73 **32**	847 41 − 316 **490**	904 269 − 79 **556**	798 280 − 142 **376**	359 90 − 21 **248**	740 380 − 242 **118**	867 329 − 415 **123**

		Addition and Subtraction Drills Answer Key				
76 + 15 **91**	34 + 76 **110**	54 − 14 **40**	90 − 32 **58**	86 + 55 **141**	86 − 55 **31**	99 − 33 **66**
67 − 31 **36**	89 + 41 **130**	76 − 66 **10**	54 − 31 **23**	22 + 16 **38**	87 − 59 **28**	33 + 99 **132**
66 + 42 = **108**	31 − 27 = **4**	54 − 29 = **25**	49 + 96 = **145**	38 + 57 = **95**	27 + 64 = **91**	75 − 35 = **40**
52 − 36 = **16**	96 − 43 = **53**	21 + 68 = **89**	53 + 94 = **147**	92 − 61 = **31**	42 + 53 = **95**	49 + 77 = **126**
67 **+ 15** 82	72 **− 59** 13	32 **+ 32** 64	**32** + 67 99	**88** − 76 12	32 − **11** 21	34 + 21 55
74 **− 38** 36	64 + 22 86	77 + 31 **108**	**70** − 23 47	39 + 32 71	72 − 64 8	54 + 23 77
341 − 142 **199**	529 + 671 **1200**	904 − 731 **173**	641 − 232 **409**	804 + 321 **1125**	922 − 344 **578**	798 + 421 **1219**
525 − 321 **204**	145 + **923** 1068	259 − 247 **12**	934 + 817 **1751**	**224** + 378 602	717 − 439 278	156 + 341 497
32 + 64 − 25 **71**	78 − 29 + 93 **142**	65 + 31 − 19 **77**	90 + 22 − 78 **34**	320 − 245 + 980 **1055**	975 − 629 + 528 **874**	802 − 492 + 375 **685**

Multiplication Drills Answer Key

6 × 8 = **48**	9 × 6 = **54**	3 × 4 = **12**	2 × 12 = **24**	5 × 9 = **45**	3 × 6 = **18**	7 × 12 = **84**
3 × 7 = **21**	6 × 3 = **18**	2 × 7 = **14**	6 × 0 = **0**	8 × 2 = **16**	7 × 9 = **63**	5 × 4 = **20**
9 × 5 = **45**	8 × 4 = **32**	4 × 7 = **28**	12 × 8 = **96**	10 × 5 = **50**	11 × 3 = **33**	6 × 4 = **24**
12 × 11 = **132**	3 × 9 = **27**	4 × 9 = **36**	5 × 3 = **15**	11 × 9 = **99**	2 × 8 = **16**	7 × 7 = **49**
6 × 2 = **12**	12 × 9 = **108**	8 × 8 = **64**	8 × 7 = **56**	12 × 4 = **48**	9 × 9 = **81**	10 × 6 = **60**
19 × 4 **76**	22 × 9 **198**	35 × 7 **245**	76 × 3 **228**	38 × 8 **304**	24 × 6 **144**	65 × 2 **130**
53 × 97 **5141**	86 × 51 **4386**	63 × 54 **3402**	11 × 22 **242**	59 × 77 **4543**	20 × 65 **1300**	95 × 38 **3610**
477 × 7 **3339**	904 × 3 **2712**	285 × 8 **2280**	876 × 9 **7884**	337 × 5 **1685**	273 × 4 **1092**	489 × 6 **2934**
395 × 44 **17380**	411 × 97 **39867**	530 × 64 **33920**	214 × 55 **11770**	503 × 84 **42252**	375 × 70 **26250**	339 × 83 **28137**
783 × 904 **707832**	899 × 974 **875626**	318 × 814 **258852**	657 × 165 **108405**	847 × 322 **272734**	555 × 396 **219780**	286 × 862 **246532**

Division Drills Answer Key						

8 ÷ 4 = **2**	12 ÷ 6 = **2**	12 ÷ 4 = **3**	12 ÷ 3 = **4**	10 ÷ 2 = **5**	4 ÷ 2 = **2**	18 ÷ 3 = **6**
18 ÷ 6 = **3**	20 ÷ 10 = **2**	15 ÷ 3 = **5**	21 ÷ 7 = **3**	20 ÷ 5 = **4**	16 ÷ 2 = **8**	25 ÷ 5 = **5**
21 ÷ 3 = **7**	30 ÷ 5 = **6**	18 ÷ 2 = **9**	15 ÷ 5 = **3**	24 ÷ 4 = **6**	20 ÷ 4 = **5**	18 ÷ 9 = **2**
35 ÷ 5 = **7**	24 ÷ 6 = **4**	32 ÷ 4 = **8**	42 ÷ 6 = **7**	26 ÷ 2 = **13**	40 ÷ 4 = **10**	24 ÷ 8 = **3**
54 ÷ 9 = **6**	48 ÷ 8 = **6**	42 ÷ 7 = **6**	55 ÷ 5 = **11**	64 ÷ 8 = **8**	36 ÷ 6 = **6**	48 ÷ 6 = **8**
1 R=1 5)6	**2** R=1 3)7	**2** R=1 4)9	**2** R=2 4)10	**2** R=2 3)8	**4** R=1 2)9	**1** R=3 7)10
4 R=2 5)22	**6** R=2 3)20	**4** R=1 6)25	**6** R=3 6)39	**8** R=3 8)67	**8** R=2 4)34	**8** R=3 5)43
87 5)435	**254** 3)762	**65** 7)455	**49** 8)392	**126** 6)756	**374** 2)748	**79** 9)711
68 11)748	**54** 8)432	**99** 3)297	**65** 4)260	**72** 7)504	**157** 5)785	**76** 9)684

Multiplication and Division Drills Answer Key

6 ÷ 3 = **2**	6 × 3 = **18**	8 ÷ 2 = **4**	8 × 2 = **16**	36 ÷ 6 = **6**	6 × 6 = **36**	64 ÷ 8 = **8**
10 ÷ 5 = **2**	10 × 5 = **50**	9 ÷ 3 = **3**	9 × 3 = **27**	81 ÷ 9 = **9**	9 × 9 = **81**	7 × 7 = **49**
56 × 4 **224**	98 × 6 **588**	37 × 2 **74**	86 × 8 **688**	30 × 3 **90**	82 × 6 **492**	39 × 7 **273**
157 5)785	**304** 3)912	**66** 7)462	**50** 8)400	**102** 6)612	**426** 2)852	**112** 9)1008
6 R=4 5)34	**17** R=1 3)52	**2** R=5 6)17	**7** R=3 6)45	**8** R=0 8)64	**6** R=1 4)25	**10** R=2 5)52
8 × 5 = 40	9 × 7 = 63	1 × 7 = 7	0 × 9 = 0	3 × 9 = 27	6 × 8 = 48	9 × 4 = 36
42 ÷ 7 = 6	60 ÷ 12 = 5	96 ÷ 4 = 24	144 ÷ 6 = 24	12 ÷ 3 = 4	54 ÷ 9 = 6	12 ÷ 2 = 6
81 ÷ 9 = 9	7 × 8 = 56	9 × 4 = 36	3 × 12 = 36	42 ÷ 7 = 6	6 × 3 = 18	40 ÷ 5 = 8
744 × 72 **53568**	843 × 21 **17703**	904 × 50 **45200**	371 × 52 **19292**	987 × 47 **46389**	382 × 82 **31324**	426 × 18 **7668**

Section 2: Factors and Multiples (Pages 75-76)

1. 2, 4, 6, 8
2. 7, 14, 21, 28, 35
3. 1, 2, 5, 10
4. 1, 2, 3, 4, 6, 8, 12, 16, 24, 48
5. 11, 13, 17, 19
6. Yes
7. Yes
8. No
9. No
10. 1

11. 2
12. 0
13. 2, 3, 3
14. 2, 17
15. 2, 2, 3, 7
16. 9
17. 1
18. 30
19. 15
20. 3

Section 3: Fractions (Pages 82-84)

1. $\dfrac{1}{3}$

2. $\dfrac{3}{8}$

3. $\dfrac{9}{12}$

4. $\dfrac{15}{25}$

5. $\dfrac{12}{7}, \dfrac{9}{7}, \dfrac{4}{7}, \dfrac{1}{7}$

6. $\dfrac{5}{2}, \dfrac{5}{3}, \dfrac{5}{6}, \dfrac{5}{8}$

7. $\dfrac{12}{8}, \dfrac{10}{8}, \dfrac{4}{8}, \dfrac{1}{8}$

8. $\dfrac{3}{2}, \dfrac{3}{3}, \dfrac{3}{7}, \dfrac{3}{8}$

9. $\dfrac{7}{10}$

10. $\dfrac{3}{5}$

11. $\dfrac{22}{15}$ or $1\dfrac{7}{15}$

12. $\dfrac{26}{15}$ or $1\dfrac{11}{15}$

13. $\dfrac{3}{10}$

14. $\dfrac{5}{36}$

15. $\dfrac{23}{12}$ or $1\dfrac{11}{12}$

16. $\dfrac{5}{3}$

17. $\dfrac{22}{7}$

18. $3\dfrac{1}{3}$

19. $1\dfrac{4}{5}$

20. $\dfrac{3}{32}$

21. $\dfrac{15}{16}$

22. $\dfrac{15}{4}$

23. $\dfrac{4}{5}$

24. $\dfrac{17}{7}$ or $2\dfrac{3}{7}$

Section 4: Ratios (Pages 88-89)

1. $\dfrac{2}{3}$

2. $\dfrac{1}{9}$

3. $\dfrac{3}{20}$

4. $\dfrac{1}{4}$

5. $\dfrac{5}{8}$

6. 330 students

7. 9 cups

8. $\dfrac{1}{2}$

9. $\dfrac{4}{9}$

10. 18 marbles

11. 54 marbles

12. 91.44 cm

13. $8

14. 12 cm

15. 2.4 packets

16. $26\dfrac{2}{3}$ pages

17. 2 kg

18. $50,000

Section 5: Decimals (Pages 95-96)

1. 6

2. 8.35

3. 6.38

4. 16.095

5. 1.28

6. 5.355

7. 26.8

8. 46.2

9. 5

10. 0.05

11. 28.644

12. 6

13. 4.2

14. 29.1

15. 3189.5

16. 41.0

17. 58000

18. 75000

19. 1000

20. 0.875

21. 0.18

22. 0.12

23. 0.475

24. $\dfrac{1}{4}$

25. $\dfrac{3}{5}$

26. $\dfrac{7}{20}$

Section 6: Percents (Pages 102-103)

1. $\dfrac{3}{5}$

2. 0.37

3. $\dfrac{17}{20}$

4. 0.29

5. 73%

6. 32.6%

7. 60%

8. 44%

9. 62.5%

10. 36

11. 63

12. 111

13. 75

14. 45%

15. 30%

16. 18 students

17. $12.30

18. 90 jelly beans

19. 50 questions

20. $200

Section 7: Word Problems (Pages 110-111)

1. 12:07PM

2. 1 hour 39 minutes

3. 7:45AM

4. $5.03

5. $11.22

6. $2.13

7. $28.55

8. Possible solution: 1 quarter, 2 dimes

9. Possible solution: 2 dollars, 6 dimes, 4 pennies

10. Possible solution: 1 dollar, 3 pennies

11. Possible solution: 3 dollars, 2 quarters, 7 pennies

12. $18.00

13. 4

14. $24

15. 37

16. 25,000 g

17. 0.478 l

18. 94

19. 57

20. 8

21. 81

22. 18

Section 8: Negative Numbers (Pages 116-117)

1. −2

2. −10

3. −11

4. 12

5. −7

6. −70

7. 18

8. −6

9. 0

10. 8000

11. −18

12. 35

13. −6

14. −40

15. −9

16. 8

17. −24

18. 15

19. −6

20. 100

Section 9: Exponents and Roots (Pages 122-123)

1. 49
2. 16
3. 125
4. 1
5. $\dfrac{8}{27}$
6. $\dfrac{1}{16}$
7. -1000
8. 81
9. 10
10. 6
11. 2
12. 4
13. $\dfrac{2}{3}$
14. $\dfrac{1}{7}$
15. 2^7, or 128
16. 5^2, or 25
17. $\left(\dfrac{1}{3}\right)^5$, or $\dfrac{1}{243}$
18. 4^4, or 256
19. 2^{12}, or 4096
20. $5\sqrt{5}$
21. $\sqrt{2}$
22. $\sqrt{9}$, or 3
23. $4\sqrt{36}$, or 24
24. 9

Section 10: Order of Operations (Pages 126-127)

1. 33
2. 13
3. 76
4. 43
5. 0
6. 34
7. 196
8. -16
9. 1
10. 9
11. 7
12. 6
13. $\dfrac{2}{9}$
14. 0
15. 5
16. 1
17. -17
18. $\dfrac{5}{4}$ or $1\dfrac{1}{4}$

1.	C	11.	E	21.	D	31.	D	41.	C
2.	B	12.	D	22.	B	32.	C	42.	D
3.	A	13.	A	23.	D	33.	D	43.	C
4.	A	14.	E	24.	E	34.	C	44.	E
5.	D	15.	C	25.	C	35.	A	45.	D
6.	C	16.	D	26.	E	36.	D	46.	C
7.	B	17.	D	27.	D	37.	C	47.	B
8.	C	18.	A	28.	C	38.	D	48.	E
9.	D	19.	E	29.	B	39.	D	49.	B
10.	B	20.	A	30.	B	40.	B	50.	A

Algebra

Section 1: Basic Algebra (Pages 146-147)

1. 10
2. 13
3. 27
4. 0
5. 8
6. 12
7. 5
8. 6
9. 20
10. 4
11. 8

12. 10
13. 2
14. 2
15. 18
16. 12
17. 6
18. 9
19. 3
20. 14
21. 4
22. 5

Section 2: Expressions (Pages 154-155)

1. 11
2. −4
3. 22
4. 18
5. $5N$
6. $9x$
7. $2a^2$
8. $h + 7$
9. $3N + M$
10. $x^2 + 3y^2$
11. $3x^2 + 36$

12. $2a^2 - 4a + 6b^2$
13. $2x^3 + 8x^2$
14. $15y^3 - 10y^2 + 50y$
15. $g + 3$
16. $4x + 6$
17. $x^2 + 7x + 10$
18. $y^2 + 6y - 40$
19. $3a^2 + 25a + 8$
20. $4x^2 - 7xy - 2y^2$
21. $4(4y + z)$
22. $3x(4x^2 + x - 3)$

Section 3: Equations (Pages 160-161)

1. $x = 36$
2. $x = 8$
3. $x = -7$
4. $x = -9$
5. $x = 12$
6. $x = 2$
7. $x = 10$
8. $x = 3$
9. $x = 5$
10. $x = -6$
11. $x = 11$
12. $x = -14$
13. $x = 9$
14. $x = 3$
15. $x = -30$
16. $x = 10$
17. $x = 24$
18. $x = 8$
19. $x = 7$
20. $x = 4$

Section 4: Inequalities (Pages 167-168)

1. Yes
2. No
3. Yes
4. Yes
5. Many possible answers greater than or equal to 10
6. Many possible answers less than 14
7. Many possible answers between 3 and 13
8. Many possible answers less than or equal to 4
9. Many possible answers greater than or equal to 7
10. Many possible answers greater than 9
11. $x \geq 3$
12. $x > 12$
13. $x \leq -1$
14. $x > -15$
15. $x > 2$
16. $x \geq 7$
17. $x > 5$
18. $x \leq -3$
19. $4 < x < 6$
20. $3 \leq x \leq 5$

Section 5: Strange Symbols (Pages 171-172)

1. 37
2. 39
3. 31
4. 20
5. 12
6. -12
7. 4
8. 60
9. 5
10. 8
11. 14
12. -2
13. 101
14. 2
15. 4
16. 45
17. $\dfrac{3}{2}$

Section 6: Word Problems and Algebra (Pages 176-178)

1. 5
2. 8
3. 14 marbles
4. 240 miles
5. $5.30
6. C
7. $30.09
8. 14
9. 4 hours and 15 minutes
10. D
11. 17 years old
12. 50 minutes, or $\frac{5}{6}$ hour
13. $15.50
14. 6 hours
15. 48 hours
16. 180
17. 12 million
18. 5 pencils

Algebra Review (Pages 179-190)

1. C	11. C	21. E	31. C	41. D
2. C	12. D	22. D	32. A	42. C
3. B	13. C	23. D	33. D	43. A
4. D	14. B	24. A	34. C	44. B
5. B	15. D	25. E	35. D	45. A
6. E	16. C	26. C	36. D	46. B
7. A	17. A	27. B	37. C	47. E
8. C	18. B	28. C	38. B	48. D
9. E	19. E	29. B	39. A	49. A
10. E	20. D	30. E	40. E	50. D

Geometry

Section 1: Lines and Angles (Pages 199-203)

1. 2
2. 8
3. 6
4. 70°
5. 20°
6. 120°
7. 55°
8. 60°
9. 60°
10. 130°
11. 30°
12. 70°
13. 60°
14. 50°
15. 50°
16. 360°
17. 35°
18. 30°

Section 2: Polygons (Pages 213-218)

1. 9.5
2. 26
3. 6
4. 25
5. 30
6. 600
7. 19
8. 81
9. 8
10. 45
11. 8 inches
12. 56
13. 48
14. 30
15. 3
16. 60°
17. 50°
18. 35°
19. 45°
20. 5
21. 6
22. 10

Section 3: Circles (Pages 221-224)

1. 6 inches
2. 10 centimeters
3. 13
4. 24
5. 8
6. 30
7. 36
8. 8
9. 16π square meters
10. 10π inches
11. 64π
12. 14
13. 18π
14. 36
15. 20π
16. 18π square feet
17. 14π inches
18. $100-25\pi$

Section 4: Solid Geometry (Pages 234-237)

1. 30
2. 64
3. 3ft
4. 3 m
5. 216 in^2
6. 15
7. 166
8. 396 ft^2
9. 30
10. 3
11. 144 m^2
12. 300 boxes
13. 1080 in^3
14. 125 cm^3
15. 125 cm^3
16. 24π
17. 130π cm^2
18. 100π cm^2
19. 8π in^3
20. 9.5π in^2

Section 5: Coordinate Geometry (Pages 249-254)

1. E
2. B and C
3. D
4. (–2, 3)
5. (1, 3)
6. P
7. 5
8. 4th
9. 5
10. (4, –1)
11. (–5, 4)
12. 6
13. 4
14. 12
15. 3
16. B
17. B
18. 10
19. 20
20. 16

Geometry Review (Pages 255-269)

1. A	11. D	21. C	31. B	41. B
2. D	12. C	22. D	32. E	42. B
3. B	13. B	23. E	33. A	43. C
4. D	14. A	24. C	34. B	44. C
5. C	15. C	25. E	35. E	45. D
6. D	16. E	26. B	36. B	46. B
7. E	17. A	27. C	37. D	47. B
8. D	18. A	28. D	38. A	48. E
9. A	19. C	29. E	39. A	49. A
10. D	20. B	30. B	40. C	50. C

Data Interpretation

Section 1: Charts and Graphs (Pages 278-283)

1. Basketball and hockey
2. 150 students
3. 32 boxes
4. $4
5. Chocolate chip and oatmeal raisin
6. 4 boxes
7. 25%
8. $180
9. Posters and Music
10. $30
11. February
12. City C
13. March
14. About 4.5 inches
15. 100 newspapers
16. About 15 newspapers
17. 7:00 – 7:15am
18. During the second half
19. Glendale County
20. $6,000

Section 2: Range, Mean, Median, and Mode (Pages 289-291)

1. $2.80
2. $2.50
3. $2.40
4. $1.20
5. 3.5 min.
6. 51 min.
7. 50.5 min.
8. 50 min.
9. 50.5 min.
10. 12 boys
11. 25 students
12. 4 students
13. 1 girl
14. 48
15. 1 book
16. 99
17. 6
18. $740
19. 31
20. 11 years old

Section 3: Probability (Pages 300-302)

1. $\dfrac{6}{13}$

2. $\dfrac{1}{4}$

3. 1

4. $\dfrac{3}{5}$

5. 12 donuts

6. $\dfrac{1}{30}$

7. $\dfrac{2}{3}$

8. $\dfrac{4}{5}$

9. $\dfrac{1}{2}$

10. $\dfrac{3}{4}$

11. 0

12. $\dfrac{1}{16}$

13. $\dfrac{1}{10}$

14. $\dfrac{1}{36}$

15. $\dfrac{3}{13}$

16. 16%

17. $\dfrac{3}{95}$

18. $\dfrac{1}{81}$

19. $\dfrac{4}{17}$

20. $\dfrac{1}{16}$

Data Interpretation Review (Pages 303-320)

1. C	11. A	21. A	31. D	41. B
2. E	12. B	22. B	32. D	42. C
3. D	13. B	23. E	33. B	43. D
4. B	14. B	24. C	34. E	44. E
5. C	15. C	25. B	35. C	45. D
6. B	16. B	26. C	36. E	46. B
7. E	17. C	27. B	37. C	47. A
8. D	18. D	28. E	38. D	48. B
9. E	19. A	29. C	39. D	49. C
10. E	20. B	30. A	40. D	50. E

Made in the USA
Columbia, SC
18 September 2018